Public Religion
in
American
Culture

PUBLIC RELIGION IN AMERICAN CULTURE

John F. Wilson

TEMPLE UNIVERSITY PRESS

PHILADELPHIA

For my father,
Frederick Colburn Wilson,
and in memory of my mother,
Esther Ryerson Gregory

Temple University Press, Philadelphia 19122
© 1979 by Temple University. All rights reserved
Published 1979
Printed in the United States of America

Library of Congress Cataloging in Publication Data

Wilson, John Frederick.
Public religion in American culture.

Includes bibliographical references and index.
1. Christianity—United States.   2. United States—
Religion.   I. Title.
BR515.W54   277.3   79-10611
ISBN 0-87722-159-6 cl; ISBN 0-87722-226-6 pbk

Contents

Preface

This book was written in response to the suggestion that I develop a sustained essay on the subject of civil religion in our society. In certain respects it has turned out to be a very private undertaking. Although I have worked upon it for some years, progress has been fitful. Innumerable professional interruptions certainly contributed to its long gestation, but more fundamental reasons also existed. The topic proved to be at once highly suggestive and exasperatingly elusive. When, on the one hand, I attempted to use to advantage the range and power of civil religion as a construction to organize historical materials, it either dissolved or appeared to be wholly artificial. When, on the other hand, the concept was refined, resolved, or reduced to essentials, it seemed to verge on the trivial. Thus in one respect the present monograph is an attempt to sort out the numerous aspects of the topic for my own benefit, so that I might lay to rest a problem that has persisted as one of my intellectual concerns for a decade.

In addition, the book is personal in a somewhat different sense. It is written as a working manual, which turns to issues in the order in which they seem to have operational importance and not necessarily as they would be synthesized in a comprehensive presentation of the subject. In this sense the book may be of special interest to other students of the very mixed religious materials of the American present and past.

However personal these concerns may have been, they are professional as well for a very good reason. While the interpretation of religion in American culture has been a vital field of scholarly research and teaching for the last several decades, there is consensus that different paradigms may now be required, that new interpretive concepts and frameworks must be fostered. Much interest has been prompted by the Civil Religion proposal because it seems so promising in just these broader respects. In this perspective the study is an inquiry into the utility of Public Religion—my preferred term, for reasons that will become clear—as a working concept for students of American religious history. As this last agenda is not at all private, although it does remain personal, this study should be of direct and general interest to others.

In light of these considerations it will be readily apparent what this study is not. These chapters are not a chronicle of Public Religion in American history and culture. If a sufficiently full and differentiated concept were articulated, no doubt such an account could be written. But it must be emphasized that this monograph is not the attempt to compose such an account.

Nor is this study a broader interpretation of American religious history from the point of view of Public Religion. Such a reinterpretation has been suggested either as a comprehensive substitute for current interpretations, or as one of several parallel projects that together would constitute a new approach to American religious history. Such a new perspective has seemed attractive as a means to overcome the strong Protestant, indeed Puritan-Protestant, bias in the interpretation of religion in America. (In this connection one might observe that the Civil Religion proposal, as it has been developed, continues in a covert fashion the Protestant bias which it ostensibly promises to overcome.) Doubtless such a program can be discharged but, no less than a history of Public Religion in America, to be adequately accomplished it would need to be predicated upon clarification and delimitation of the controlling concept. That latter task is the chief burden of this monograph.

Accordingly the most significant aspect of the project is that it amounts to an argument (through an example) that reflective analysis about constructs is prerequisite to development of the study of American religious history. In that sense, and offered very much as a self-consciously chosen example of what needs to be done with various other interpretive constructs, the monograph represents a declaration or argument entered for consideration within professional discussions.

As indicated by the table of contents the study moves *toward* conclusions, if it does not reach them in a definitive sense. Thus the Public Religion question will remain under discussion throughout the study even as it is at the beginning. In the course of the analysis, however, the topic should have ramified and become more complex by virtue of continuing introduction of additional considerations and critical perspectives.

Numerous friends and associates helped me in writing and revising this analysis of a complex issue. In particular Martin E. Marty, John M. Mulder, and Benjamin C. Ray encouraged the project and gave helpful criticisms at different important points. I appreciate their assistance in moving my discussion beyond positions I had previously set out in various essays so as to achieve a more comprehensive view of the subject. My debt to several others should also be acknowledged. Viviette Allen, Mary Forsythe, Lorraine Fuhrmann, Patricia Halliday, and Carol Roan all gave me extensive help. Especially Leonard V. Galla provided critical assistance. Of course I must be held responsible for the direction and the particulars of the study.

Thanksgiving Day, 1978
Princeton, N.J.

Public Religion
in
American
Culture

Chapter 1

PUBLIC RELIGION
AS AN AMERICAN PROBLEM

In a little-known private letter composed at the end of his
life, James Madison, who had been instrumental in the
founding and development of the new American nation,
reflected upon a subject which had concerned him
throughout his career. He was responding to the Reverend
Jasper Adams, at the time president of Charleston College
in South Carolina, who had sent the former President a
copy of his convention sermon, "The Relation of Christianity to Civil Government in the United States." In trans-
mitting the text, he had asked for Madison's comments on
his effort. This request occasioned a discussion by Madison
of the ancient problem of the relationship between religion
and government and the particular solution arrived at in
the new American Republic. In brief comments he lined
out the various patterns of church-state relationships
which European states had adopted. "The prevailing opinion in Europe, England not excepted, has been that
Religion could not be preserved without the support of
Government nor Government supported without an established religion[,] that there must be at least an alliance
of some part between them." Madison believed that "It remained for North America to bring the great & interesting
subject to a fair, and finally to a decisive test."[1]

Madison briefly reviewed the kinds of "experiments"
made in the several colonies, calling special attention to the

case of Virginia, where the decision concerning disestablishment of the Church of England permitted a direct comparison between the experience of establishment and that of absolute religious freedom under nonestablishment. Acknowledging that other factors in addition to the religious one certainly were present, he nonetheless believed that the experience of fifty years allowed significant conclusions to be drawn which were of more than local importance. In brief, under the conditions that religious institutions were independent of civil government and that religious freedom was assured, religion had flourished and civil government had survived. "Religion . . . does not need the support of Government and it will scarcely be contended that Government has suffered by the exemption of Religion from its cognizance, or its pecuniary aid."[2]

Madison was aware of possible complexities in this new American arrangement of the church-state issue. He acknowledged, for instance, that without control religion "may run into extravagances injurious both to [itself] and to social order." But he thought that government interference might "more likely . . . increase [rather] than control the tendency" and that reason would reassert itself in any case. He also opined that under conditions of self-support religion would not likely suffer from lack thereof. On the contrary religious institutions, without limitations on the duration of charities, might accumulate so much wealth ["prompted by a pious zeal or by an atoning remorse"] as to threaten the social order. Further, Madison admitted that "it may not be easy, in every possible case, to trace the line of separation between the rights of religion and the Civil authority with such distinctness as to avoid collisions & doubts on unessential points." Nonetheless, he held to the main point which he thought proved by the American experience:

The tendency to a usurpation on one side or the other, or to a corrupting coalition or alliance between them, will best be guarded against by an entire abstinance of the Government from interference in any way whatever, beyond the necessity of preserving public order, & protecting each sect against trespasses on its legal rights by others.[3]

Madison's letter deserves to have been more widely known and used as an explanation of his intentions as he participated in the Virginia struggle for disestablishment. It also illuminates the decisive role he played in shaping the Federal Constitution and the Bill of Rights. In the absence of his rather subtle and rich insights into what had been wrought in the American experiment with the classical church-state issue, we have been at the mercy of simplistic formulas. A good example of the latter is Thomas Jefferson's "Wall of Separation."[4] Such metaphors are misleading because they misrepresent intentions underlying the resolution of social issues, as well as actual results. Madison's sage counsel derived from his appreciation that both religious institutions and civil governments could better serve their purposes if each was not trammeled by the other. In this sense, the dissolving of a historic tie between churches and states promised that each would in some measure be transformed. That was the significance of the experiment taking place in North America.

In the many decades since Madison composed his response to Jasper Adams, the church-state question has been widely discussed in the public realm, argued in court, and analyzed by partisans and scholars. This essay is not another attempt to return to that issue but an effort to push beyond it. Essentially, Madison was correct that the American polity would be committed simultaneously to religious freedom for all and to the disengagement of religious institutions from civil governments. He was also correct in recognizing that to draw a line between them adequate to cover all cases would be extremely difficult. The church-state conflicts and discussions of succeeding years have basically concerned the drawing of that line, however, rather than repudiating or revising the basic premise. Religious observances in schools and public places, public funding of different kinds of nonreligious activities at basically religious colleges, tax policy with respect to income-producing, church-owned property— the list is very long and filled with very particular issues. But all of the issues have been occasion to trace or give definition to that *line* rather than to call into question the American pattern. Madison's counsel is markedly more helpful in comprehending this grand experiment than Jefferson's casually delivered unyielding metaphor, which has perhaps finally obscured more than it has clarified this area.

After paying such tribute to Madison's insight, however, it may in turn be criticized for its limitations, especially for its failure to recognize other levels of the relationship between religion and government than those properly comprehended under the church-state rubric. Madison was basically concerned with institutional arrangements, provisions for the terms in which individual religious bodies and particular civil governments might interact. Beneath the level where this pattern of interaction between institutions has proved durable, so to speak, are other levels at which public issues have not been so readily segregated from religious values. The proper distinction to be developed is not between an institutional (collective) level and a valuational (individual) level, although numerous attempts have been made to superimpose these separate classification systems. The point is that issues of concern to the public are not only of concern to individuals as individuals but are also of concern to them as they are members of groups. This means that religious values are held in common and express the collective goals of groups even as they are embraced by individuals. In modern terms religion and politics interact in a social setting, so that culture is the medium in which resolution of tensions is expressed. This deeper level of mutual influence did not altogether elude Madison, it seems, but he appears to have discounted its significance.

The formative and shaping influence of religion within the American (as any) society has been repeatedly recognized over the course of the national history. Benjamin Franklin, among the founding fathers, may have been the earliest to advocate serious attention to the public import of religion. In his 1749 "Proposals" he urged the founding of an academy in Philadelphia for the education of youth (proposals which stand behind the institution which became the University of Pennsylvania). He took special note of the "useful" and "ornamental" studies in which youth ought to be engaged.[5] Among these, "history" was important, for through such studies youth are, to use our term, acculturated. Franklin thought that one reason among others for the study of history was that it would

afford frequent Opportunities of showing the Necessity of a *Publick Religion,* from its Usefulness to the Publick; the Advantages of a Religious Character among private Persons; the Mischiefs of Superstition, &c. and the Excellency of the CHRISTIAN RELIGION above all others antient or modern.[6]

It is not immediately clear from this passage whether

7

Franklin intended to argue that a specific religion is necessary to the existence of each particular public realm, or whether his reference is to the role played by any broadly based religion with respect to fostering the quality of public life. The form of the proposals as a whole, and comparison with other specific paragraphs, suggests this latter construction as the proper one. Franklin seems not to argue that each society has its own positive religion directly focused on the public realm. He does appear to claim that one may infer from history that the popular religion of a society makes important contributions in terms of forming citizens and shaping the common life.

This observation was not, of course, terribly innovative. The line of argument has an ancient origin in the West and was re-expressed in the territorial pattern of religious life adopted in European lands in the preceding centuries. For our purposes the interesting question is what happened to that cultural assumption when formal separation between religious institutions and civil governments took place in America between 1782 and 1832. Occasional intellectuals may have anticipated the development of a religiously plural culture, even one we might term "secular," as the natural outcome of these conditions—that is, a public realm in which there was no fundamental consensus in religious terms. Such, for example, is an interpretation which can be placed upon the philosophical reflections of Jefferson and his circle.[7] For most advocates of rational religion, however, the more likely outcome would be a nonestablished religious culture free of superstition and rooted in reason. Benign influence would be suffused throughout the public realm by means of enlightened religious values widely shared among the citizens of the republic.[8]

Such a vision was anathema to more evangelical types of

Protestants. They perceived that, sooner or later, disestablishment, the severing of their dependent relationship on government, would open new possibilities for them. It had actually liberated religious bodies to work assertively within the common life. This not only made it possible to organize strong religious congregations, and groups of congregations into denominations as well, disestablishment also led to systematic attempts to exert influence on the public realm. This influence consisted generally of a suffusion of Christian values and goals into the society, but more specifically of concerted actions on behalf of particular projects. Franklin's historical moral that there was a "necessity" for a "public religion"—that is, for religion to influence the realm of public (in contrast to private) life—seemed fulfilled by the project to make America a Christian nation in substance if not in law.

This bold strategy on the part of the evangelicals and the tactics employed to achieve it have been critically discussed in numerous modern studies. Some of their titles graphically suggest the cultural reality which expressed this republican Protestant ideal: Ernest Lee Tuveson, *Redeemer Nation;*[9] Martin E. Marty, *Righteous Empire;*[10] Robert T. Handy, *A Christian America.*[11] A long series of monographs has delineated one or another aspect of the complex of nineteenth-century Protestant denominations and movements.[12] Republican Protestantism, which constituted a coherent culture, directly confirmed the moral Ben Franklin drew from history: "The Necessity of a Publick Religion." Franklin's assumption about public religion remained vital to the evangelical strategy in the nineteenth century. For example, Associate Justice of the Supreme Court Joseph Story, who was deeply influential in the development of the American legal tradition, interpreted the religion clauses of the Bill of Rights in just such terms.[13] "The promulgation of the great doctrines of religion . . . one Almighty God; the responsibility to him for all our actions. . . ; a future state of rewards and punishments; the cultivation of all the personal, social, and benevolent virtues;—these never can be a matter of indifference in any well-ordered community. It is, indeed, difficult to conceive, how any civilized society can well exist without them." Story went on to opine that "in a republic, there would seem to be a peculiar propriety in viewing the Christian religion, as the great basis, on which it must rest for its support and permanence. . . ."

That these were not idiosyncratic American judgments is clear. The influence and significance of Christianity as a cultural reality in the new nation was obvious to visitors who commented upon it. Francis Grund, for one, who immigrated to the United States from Austria in 1827, reflected upon the peculiar place of religion in his new homeland. He concluded that "the religious habits of the Americans form not only the basis of their private and public morals, but have become so thoroughly interwoven with their whole course of legislation, that it would be impossible to change them without affecting the very essence of their government."[14] Grund thought that "the Americans look upon religion as a promoter of civil and political liberty; and have, therefore, transferred to it a large portion of the affection which they cherish for the institutions of their country."[15] In Grund's eyes the relationship between religion and morality was especially close, and both directly influenced life in the public realm. "Public virtue must be guarded against the pernicious influence of example; vice must be obliged to conceal itself, in order not to tincture society in general. In this consists the true force and wholesome influence of public opinion. It becomes a mighty police-agent of morality and religion, which not only discovers crimes, but partly prevents their commission."[16]

The most celebrated account of America written for Europeans was produced by Alexis de Tocqueville. Many aspects of American religious life intrigued the French student of American penal institutions. Especially, he was convinced that in the large framework Roman Catholic Christianity was not at all antithetic to democracy. Indeed, he thought that because of its emphasis upon equality in the sight of God, the ancient church might provide basic support for the new republic.[17] Tocqueville observed that "Religion in America takes no direct part in the government of society, but [nevertheless] it must be regarded as the first of their political institutions; for . . . it facilitates the use of [freedom]; . . . I do not know whether all Americans have a sincere faith in their religion—for who can search the human heart?—but I am certain that they hold it to be indispensable to the maintenance of republican institutions."[18]

The line of thought was carried further by an English Methodist, James Dixon, who toured the United States in 1848. He thought that, given the opportunity of a *tabula rasa,* the American people were "disposed to adopt a new principle."[19] This was to discard "all authoritative church-organization" and to try "the effect of Christianity itself, in its own native grandeur and divine simplicity." Dixon thought that the Bible had become the "governing light, the decisive authority, the court of final appeal." "All the interests of society converge to this point; religion is its life, its power, its beauty. It is like the *substrata* of the world, on which all the soils whence the vegetable productions spring repose in security." In what now appears to have been ominous foreboding (the Methodist church had already split along sectional lines in 1844) Dixon asked: "Is this common Christianity, taught and developed in Scripture, sufficient for a nation? May the people of a state be safely left, other things being favourable, to this simple process? The answer to this question is in course of solution in the United States."[20]

Insofar as the American republic was viewed as the pure political expression of Christianity, making of the latter its "public religion," an irreconcilable moral tension existed between, on the one hand, the universalism of the gospel together with the liberty it promised and, on the other, the great slave-holding society of the southern states which systematically held humans in bondage. Chesterton's felicitous phrase about the "nation with the soul of a church"[21] identifies perfectly the kinds of moral tensions experienced all the more intensely in the practical world as a result of this confusion of categories. Because there was no separation of public religion from government, Americans had no recourse during a bloody Civil War to an alternate society (the church). Only in such a separate institution might there have been discussion of another realm in which the ambiguities and sufferings of this world were possibly reconciled with true morality. The nation *was* the church and as the churches had split along sectional lines a decade or more before so the nation must suffer as a flawed moral community.

Without such an understanding of the public import of Christianity to the American republic it is impossible to grasp the role played by Abraham Lincoln. At once, he profoundly articulated the moral dilemmas of the nation, made of the Union a virtually mystical cause, and finally, in his death, served as a symbolic propitiation for the evil which was thus vanquished. At few times in history have public officeholders risen to such heights of self-understanding to articulate the cultural meaning of their

deeds and finally death.[22] In his death there is a conjunc-
tion between, on the one hand, the Biblical symbols and
Christian religion that suffused the republic's culture and,
on the other, the traumatic civil struggle within the
society. Out of this experience the American nation issued
forth upon the historical stage of modernity.[23]

It might be thought that the civil struggle, however
sanctified to the nation, might finally have brought to an
end the role of Protestant Christianity as the public
religion of the American society. Far from it. Philip Schaff,
writing for the recently founded American Historical
Association at the end of his long career, summarized the
American dependence on Christianity. "Christianity is the
most powerful factor in our society and the pillar of our
institutions. It regulates the family; it enjoins private and
public virtue; it builds up moral character; it teaches us to
love God supremely, and our neighbor as ourselves; it
makes good men and useful citizens; it denounces every
vice; it encourages every virtue; it promotes and serves the
public welfare; it upholds peace and order. Christianity is
the only possible religion for the American people, and
with Christianity are bound up all our hopes for the
future."[24] If for Schaff Christianity was the "regulator" of
life, for James Bryce it was no less the center of national
life: "Christianity is in fact understood to be, though not
the legally established religion, yet the national religion. So
far from thinking the commonwealth godless, the Americans conceive that the religious character of a government
consists in nothing but the religious belief of individual
citizens, and the conformity of their conduct to that belief.
They deem the general acceptance of Christianity to be
one of the main sources of their national prosperity, and
their nation a special object of Divine favour."[25] Throughout the nineteenth century informed observers believed

that Christianity served America as that public religion which Franklin had thought necessary for any polity. What had been proved in the American experiment was certainly not that the Christian religion was unimportant to the civil government, but that its contribution could, without benefit of establishment, as well be indirect and informal as explicit and legal. In the twentieth century this pattern of republican protestant Christianity was called into question.

Finally, it is not important to date precisely the end of this cultural hegemony of republican Protestantism in the public realm. Depending upon the aspect of cultural life selected, 1908 or 1958 might seem more appropriate. For at the beginning of the century the Roman Catholic Church in the United States was declared to be no longer a mission field and thus became an independent entity, while concurrently there began the development of conciliar structures among Protestant denominations which suggested a necessity for them to organize as an institution to influence the public realm in effective ways.[26] These events suggest the dissipation of that Protestant republican culture which had provided a continuous and pervasive influence within the society and upon politics. In 1958, on the other hand, the campaign began in earnest to secure the presidential nomination for Senator John F. Kennedy, who would lead the Democratic Party to victory as a Roman Catholic layman in the 1960 election. He succeeded President Eisenhower, who represented many aspects of American life—the successful soldier-statesman, the triumph of virtue over modest beginnings, and the nostalgia for an era in which rural values dominated America. In all these he stood for the hold of old-fashioned republican Protestantism upon the central ground of the national political life.

14

Between these symbolically striking events numerous others might also be chosen as significant in marking the end of the Protestant cultural hegemony as the public religion of the American nation. The failure of Woodrow Wilson's crusade to make the world safe for democracy; the ill-fated experiment with legislated prohibition of alcoholic beverages; the reconstruction of American political life under the patrician reformer Franklin Roosevelt; the emergence of the American Jewish community as co-equal with the Protestant and Catholic communities. This last example suggests how, with especial clarity during and after World War II, the public religion Franklin believed to be necessary became identified with several separate religious communities. Religious pluralism, which in a technical sense had been social reality from colonial days, at last became explicitly recognized as cultural reality.

The most broadly influential study of this new stage of public religion in America was the work of Will Herberg.[27] His *Protestant-Catholic-Jew* quickly became widely utilized and accepted as an acute analysis of religion in American public life. A number of different themes can be identified in the study. The most basic one for our purposes was that the three major faith communities (and there was no necessity that there be only three—perhaps Orthodox Christianity should be seen as a fourth, or Humanism[28]) while remaining independent were yet expressions of a spiritual reality identified by Herberg as "The American Way of Life." Herberg believed this to be a kind of "secularized Puritanism" which represented not only the basic spiritual reality of American life but also the common content expressed by the three (or four, or five) chief faith communities in slightly different form. Thus in the larger view the republican Protestantism which had been the public religion shaping the morals and sustaining the values of an earlier nation had been superseded by a religiously plural Americanism which preserved much of the same cultural content, albeit no longer as explicitly Protestant or even necessarily Christian.

It was just these latter implications which generated wide-ranging discussions of the Herberg analysis. The author had indicated what he believed to be the spiritual inadequacies of The American Way of Life.[29] He thought that biblical religion—whether in Jewish or Christian forms—finally resisted the reduction of life to *these* terms. So Will Herberg, while identifying The American Way of Life as the operative public religion, was at the same time a critic of its inadequacies as a religion. Herberg was joined in this by numerous others who lamented the erosion of specific traditions into versions of spiritual Americanism in the public realm.[30]

If religious critics of The American Way like Herberg and Martin E. Marty protested the spiritual inadequacies of this new public religion, others came to see that Way as corrupt and hypocritical. In the course of the late 1950s, following *Brown* v. *Board of Education,* and into the 1960s, a massive struggle on behalf of civil rights for *all* Americans amounted to an outright rejection of the spiritual Americanism, at least as it had been conceived. As a public religion, the Way had worked to obscure the second-class status which was the actual America known by black citizens. Further, it supported the structures of power and self-interest which gave no sign of permitting let alone encouraging change. In the 1960s this rejection merged into (and was amplified by) the internal civil struggle against the war in southeast Asia. It was possible to paraphrase Franklin's analysis and reach a negative conclusion. Current history no longer seemed to afford "opportunity of showing the necessity of a Publick Religion, from its

Usefulness to the Publick; . . . & the Excellency of the Religion of the American Way above all others antient or modern." Within the framework of the present discussion, the decade of the 1960s was at least as momentous as that of the 1860s. If civil struggle of the nineteenth century secured the unity of the nation as a religious entity—albeit with Church and State separated—the civil struggles of the twentieth century finally rendered that religious basis for unity broken and ineffective. As the nation approached the bicentennial celebration of its independence, it was for the first time manifestly plural in religion and genuinely secular in government. The spiritual mold of a public religion was broken.

Churches and governments had indeed been formally independent of each other from the outset of the American republic; that is to say, Madison's great experiment in disengaging them had been a cultural reality. But it began to appear that the 200 years of separation might have depended on the spiritual capital of Christendom. For a public religion, whether called republican Protestantism, pure Christianity, or The American Way of Life, had made possible the cultural unity which was premised by the social institutions, especially the political ones. This is the sense in which many perceived the 1960s to be the end of an era. It was not that the separate manifestations of social transformation were unparalleled or overwhelming. The list would surely include changing sexual mores, accentuated ethnic self-consciousness, new patterns in relationships among the races, and civil disobedience—the list is very long and basic. But taken together, the set of them marked a stark repudiation of that spiritual ethos which had persisted throughout the life of the nation, albeit at times more pronounced and on other occasions weakened.

This is the framework within which Sydney Ahlstrom's

emphasis upon the decisive end of a Puritan era in American history is convincing.[31] It is not that anything remotely resembling seventeenth-century colonial Puritanism had been preserved into the twentieth century. Nor is it that in the 1960s, by some standard, a decisive shift in kinds of religious allegiance had taken place, or that the religious lives of Protestants or Protestant groups had been deeply transformed. Rather, the point is that in spite of significant changes through the centuries, as in the commitment to indepence of church and state, there had remained a public religion in Franklin's sense, a synthesis including broadly religious symbols and values (which had derived from Protestant forms of Christianity) and patterns of behavior in the public realm. Thus private and public morality overwhelmingly reflected a cultural consensus that was, in Bryce's terms, the "national religion." To be sure, elements of that culture remain, and periodic attempts have been made and will be made to recreate it. But in the framework of the history of America it seems likely that a fundamental shift will be seen to have taken place, making the decade of the 1960s decisive in the cultural life of the nation.

This cultural transformation of American society in the 1960s has received attention in its own right, but it is also fascinating as a setting for analysis of a related development. It provided occasion for the proposal that there is [read "has been and ought to be"] in American society a public religion in quite another sense—the sense that public piety centered on the nation actually constitutes a particular "civil religion in America."[32] This civil religion, suggested Robert Bellah, while in one sense a dimension of American life which might be hard to distinguish from republican Protestantism or pure Christianity, or even the American way of life within American culture, was in another respect a positive religion, well-institutionalized and parallel to the variety of other specific religions in the society. Bellah thought that this phenomenon had escaped serious attention because, on the whole, the Western religions represented in the society (Judaism and Christianity) are generally nontolerating and manifestly resist syncretism, thus hiding the pluriformity in religious belief and behavior which is so much more obvious in Eastern cultures. Bellah did think that syncretism had actually proceeded far in the American case—so much so that characteristic Biblical themes and motifs had been blended with American materials to create the distinctive civil religion of the society. Actually, as this chapter has suggested, Americans have characteristically understood from the outset of national life that within their culture, some form of public religion—republican Protestantism, pure Christianity, or The American Way of Life—has served as a basic religious medium in the culture and as such has been enormously significant in the society. In this sense what led to the excited response to the civil religion proposal was a conviction, widely shared, that an effective religious medium no longer was part of the culture. In line with Bellah's suggestion, it appeared that a positive religion might be precipitated out of that medium to have an independent existence.

This possibility represented a genuinely new insight into American society; perhaps it would be more accurate to term it a genuine vision for the renewal of American society. The intent of the proposal was no less than the revitalization of the culture, specifically through its religious medium, so that in a time of global trials as the twenty-first century approached, the nation might renew, perfect, and sustain its broadly liberal commitments. So in this respect the civil religion proposal was itself a religious statement and has evoked what finally must be identified as a religious response. In this sense the proposal will finally be evaluated at a practical level retrospectively in terms of its success or failure as it proves, or fails, to contribute to the revivifying of the culture, and through it the American national life.

At a theoretical level it must, of course, be evaluated in a different framework. In one sense, that is the burden of this study. What does seem incontestable is that discussion of the question of public religion in America, which Franklin first raised among his junto in pre-Revolutionary Philadelphia, has entered a new stage. The question has been transformed to become: whether a public religion once substantially depleted in a democratic society can be revitalized. The unspoken premise, of course, is that without such a development the nation cannot long endure—at least as a republican democracy.

If we must wait for historical evidence before addressing the practical question whether civil religion can revivify the culture, there is a related question that can be reviewed immediately. Has civil religion been prominent in the sense of representing a specific, positive religion within the American society? The answer seems clear if by it we mean a well-institutionalized religion continuous across 200 years of American history. In this sense, there has not been an American civil religion. Where are those marks of differentiation within the culture and from other religions which we look for in proposing a straightforward response to this question? But there have been mythic elements within the culture amounting to a religious sanction for the national polity. Certainly, figures, places, and times sacred to the nation abound throughout our history. Symbols and images celebrating a national purpose commissioned by the diety have been commonplace together with ceremonial occasions centered on America. In sum, elements of public religious piety across generations, elements sufficient to the birth of an American civil religion, certainly have existed. It does seem clear that something like a positive religion has been fused out of these elements in particular episodes to create, if only for brief periods or for small groups, American civil cults. The founding of the nation, its sanctification through civil struggle, its rededication after the assassination of its leaders—these may be seen as particular periods in which civil religion became a significant if transient reality in America. Indeed the proposal itself that there was a civil religion in America emerged from the collective trauma of a particular national episode, that period in which the loss of public religion in the culture was decisively manifested.

In this framework it appears plausible to argue that civil religions have come into being in America and passed away again. Therefore it is not altogether out of the question to hypothesize that a more lasting American civil cult may emerge—whether to succeed in revitalizing public religion in the culture at large or to become a particular positive religion in the social matrix. Whatever the future of American civil religion in this sense, it will have been possible to raise an important issue at this point—namely, what is the set of cultural materials in which we might locate the potential for an American civil religion? Leaving open the question what hypothetical role a differentiated positive American civil religion might play, the more significant issue is cultural assumptions about the nature of religion. Western religions, as a part of their exclusivity, make the assumption that they originate *de novo,* are independent of prior materials. But it is clear that this is a religious viewpoint towards their origin, not a critical interpretation of them. In this sense the next chapters are attempts to identify the mythic materials in the culture which have to do with the nation and its religious identity —that is, its self-understanding in a cosmic frame of reference.

The agenda of the following pages follows from this analysis of our present situation. First, attention will turn to the religious materials in the public realm which pose the problem before us—the mythic materials centered on the polity which are a cultural given. A series of subsequent chapters offers systematic and formal analysis of four aspects of the culture in which evidence for civic piety is alleged to be manifest. These aspects are: (1) strictly linguistic formulations of American religious identity delivered by our presidents; (2) ritual or stylized behavior in the collective life which points toward the social reality of this democratic republic; (3) the array of "meanings" commonly attributed to the American nation; (4) the institutions which might be viewed as supporting a positive public religion or civic cult. A concluding chapter turns directly to more strictly theoretical issues of the interpretation of public religion in America. The epilogue suggests an interpretation of the civil religion proposal as a religious movement in its own right. Thus, the logic of the study flows from more empirical to more theoretical concerns, or from problems of evidence to interpretive issues. The overarching thesis is that these different kinds of questions cannot be separated and that the civil religion discussion to date has been severely flawed by failure to observe this constraint. Beyond sustaining that position, the study should establish the point, beyond reasonable doubt, that public religion in American society deserves serious attention.

Chapter 2

THE SHAPE OF
THE NATIONAL COVENANT

In the preceding chapter we identified a recent religious development in American culture: the erosion of a set of general assumptions identified as the religious aspects of the national community, or the public religion of America. Certainly the content of this public religion had not remained constant across the preceding years of national life; Will Herberg's delineation of the "American Way of Life" in the 1950s was significantly different from the pure Christianity that a century earlier James Dixon had believed to be at the center of the society. Nor was it that critics of public religion and sceptics about its status were active for the first time; Madison, to take the best example, valued the social achievement of religious pluralism as much as did any mid-twentieth century counterpart. What occurred were pronounced shifts in public attitudes and actions. In the 1960s a markedly secularized attitude toward religion came to dominate popular culture. This basic development provided the occasion for serious discussion of the civil religion question.

Concurrent with this change in popular perceptions was a shift in the understanding of religion among intellectuals. The development of social theory, following from the work of Emile Durkheim and Max Weber, entailed new ways of conceptualizing the place of religion in societies. The religious aspect of cultures came to receive unprecedented attention. If to the popular mind indifferent attitudes toward religion were increasingly commonplace, in the abstract discussions of social theoreticians religion had never seemed more relevant to the perseverance of societies and the viability of cultures. While different authors proposed distinctive formulations of the issue, the general position was broadly espoused that religions, or something very much like religious legitimations of basic patterns of belief and behavior, seem to be central to social structures. This appeared to hold for "complex" and extensive, as well as for "simple" and small-scale, societies. Although the most attractive formulations of this position diverged in particulars, the theoretical point was single and compelling: any durable society seems to possess important collective religious aspects instrumental in its achievement of coherence and in its continuing viability. Thus, the recent discussion of public religion, although occasioned by general developments in popular culture, has received its specific form and shape from contemporaneous counter-currents within essentially academic circles.

This point may be underscored by giving brief attention to several influential formulations—one by a cultural anthropologist, Clifford Geertz, and one by a sociologist, Peter Berger. The details of each version are less significant for this discussion than the broadly common insight that, to use a spatial image, religion establishes horizons for a culture, orienting the collectivity and the individuals who compose it through time and across social space. Religion sets the forms in which thought takes place and condenses the values which guide behavior. Within this framework, religion is viewed as a *condition* for culture at the same time that it is perceived in terms of a set of discrete phenomena within it.

In one influential essay, Peter Berger and his collaborator Thomas Luckmann summarized and synthesized recent discussion in the sociology of knowledge bearing on this point. *The Social Construction of Reality* argues that humans necessarily exist in a dialectical relationship with their "worlds," at once experiencing the worlds as given, while engaging in activity which recreates and sustains them.[1] In this sense, the "real" world exists only in the knowledge of it that individuals and collectivities share and reproduce. From this point of view, all kinds of knowledge—from the hard physical sciences at one extreme to realms of human creativity and meaning at the other—share common formal properties. The collaborators diverge in their interpretations at this point. Luckmann assumes that a universe of meaning is religious by virtue of its function, whether or not it makes manifest religious references.[2] Berger, by contrast, is committed to a more substantive definition of religion; in theory his position allows for "universes of meaning" not explicitly religious to arise from the social dialectic which produces and sustains each cosmos.[3]

Resolution of the point at issue between these two authors is not immediately relevant to our present inquiry, for the perception common to both is that a society acquires and maintains its legitimacy over time and through space on the basis of a meaning system which has been, empirically or historically speaking, most frequently religious. On this view we might expect to discover public religion, or cultural equivalents for it, in all social systems. "Religion legitimates social institutions by bestowing upon them an ultimately valid ontological status, that is, by *locating* them within a sacred and cosmic frame of reference."[4] In this sense, religion may be perceived as basic to or fundamental within a culture; indeed, in this respect it gives definition to a culture. Above all, this line of analysis makes clear why it is important to locate and identify the special, if not exclusive, characteristics of religion within culture.

An influential essay by Clifford Geertz is helpful at this point. "Religion as a Cultural System" indicates how certain anthropologists have come to define particular aspects of culture as religious.[5] In form, the essay is an extended exposition of a particular definition of religion. Geertz suggests at the outset that:

A religion is: (1) a system of symbols which acts to (2) establish powerful, pervasive, and long-lasting moods and motivations in men by (3) formulating conceptions of a general order of existence and (4) clothing these conceptions with such an aura of factuality that (5) the moods and motivations seem uniquely realistic.[6]

While a stipulative definition of this kind does not gain universal assent even among cultural anthropologists, the *form* of this proposal has been extremely useful in pointing to the location of religion and the specific roles attributed to religion in a culture. Further, in theory this approach may be applied to internally diverse, large-scale empires as well as to small-scale, self-contained, and relatively static societies. Finally, the thrust of this definition is not to argue that every culture embodies a religion, but to identify certain issues or problem areas common to cultures where phenomena fruitfully viewed as religious might be studied. Thus, those meanings which situate a collectivity in a cosmos and provide both general orientation and specific motivation for individual and collective behavior are at least religion-like cultural materials, if not formal religions. These structures of meaning and value are fundamentally *symbolic* rather than rational. Futhermore, rather than appear as disparate elements, they compose a coherent set, or constitute a cult.

The relevance of such an approach to analysis of public religion is obvious. The discussion of civil religion to date has exemplified how there might be located in American culture some of the materials which maintain the social and cultural systems in the ways Peter Berger and Clifford Geertz have proposed. Since religion is specific to a collectivity, it is not surprising that the relevant American materials should carry the imprint of the Biblical or Hebraic tradition so deeply influential in western societies.[7] The symbolism which predominates in this great tradition is very much historical in cast. In particular, the interpretation of change through time is the central problematic, and the direction and significance of that change is identified and expressed through emphasis upon the origin and destiny of the society, or its beginning and end. Further, the Biblical tradition is markedly realistic. Meaning is identified through dramatic figures who act out intentions common to the collectivity through particular events fraught with special significance.[8] Accordingly, change through time is not conceived passively, as it is in some cultures where the objective is endurance. Rather, it is viewed actively. Particular subjects, at propitious moments, behave in ways to move the present toward the future out of the past.

Much has been written about the concept of history stemming from the Biblical tradition and about its influence in Western culture through Judaism and Christianity.[9] Discussion of that literature in detail would not materially advance the present analysis. The basic point is that the legitimation public religion has conferred upon

American society, or the type of cosmos public religion has provided within the American cultural system, is a variant of this Western cultural pattern derived from the Bible. This observation suggests why the central symbolism of the American public religion involves myths of the national community's origin and destiny rendered concrete in terms of larger-than-life agents acting through specific events perceived as crucial. These elements, or basic symbols, set a covenantal framework for the American culture. Thus we logically turn to give attention to the basic shape and content of the myths which establish a cosmos with respect to the American nation.

The mythic center of these peculiarly American materials concern corporate destiny or purpose—in a phrase, the national covenant.[10] These materials focus the nation's self-understanding *as a collectivity.* Unquestionably, each national community develops its own sense of particular mission or destiny. Current cultural nationalisms are certainly familiar to us. There are small-scale examples from Africa's recent era of nation-building, and a universalistic case in Soviet Russia as a continental empire. That our particular nation has a strong sense of identity does not comprise the uniqueness of the American materials; there is a distinctiveness, however, in the form and content of the particular national myths. The American materials are characterized by themes which derive from a specifically Christian version of the broadly Biblical tradition. More especially, the comprehensive kingdom-tradition, or millenarian component of Christianity, figures large.[11] The national covenant has been variously conceived. The earliest version, for example, envisioned America as the beginning of the long-expected Christian millennium.[12] As a relatively direct extrapolation of a traditional view, this expectation was current among

English colonists, and it was also held by certain European circles. Alternatively, a more recent construct of the covenant was conceived in terms of the American nation's fulfilling the millennial expectation of the ages.[13] This latter is a more heretical point of view in terms of orthodox Christianity, but it has been a powerful ingredient in American nationalism. In any case, the several versions of the Kingdom myth attributed to the American community have placed the national experience in a universal framework. In all the versions America is placed at center stage in the concluding act of world history.

If this Hebraic sense of historical destiny allied with the Christian image of the millennium has provided the basic form of national identity for the American community, its manifestations have been somewhat more variable, allowing for a wide range of interpretations of the American community and its covenant. Generations of reformers have spoken in millennial terms of more perfect social orders of one sort or another. At times their focus has been political, emphasizing human rights. At other times they have been more interested in economic questions, specifically those concerning rights of property. In some ways, however, the interpretations offered are less important than the mythic patterns on which they are based. Two such patterns can be identified, and clear distinctions drawn between them. On the one hand is the exemplary pattern; on the other is the emissary.[14]

Exemplary versions of America's mission locate the central collective national purpose in America's exhibiting to the world the achievement of a perfected society. This theme, rooted in Puritan self-understanding, was classically articulated by John Winthrop in his address aboard the Arbella. The image he developed, as school children know, was that of the "City set on a hill."[15] The root theological premise is that God has chosen to make an example of a perfected society in the American wilderness for the sake of the old world. This might instruct in His true ways the warring European nations.[16] That explicit theological significance has not necessarily been central in subsequent exemplary constructions of the national mission. Among positive transformations, America has been envisioned as the land of liberty in which democracy has replaced perfected Christian society.[17]

Exemplary constructions have entailed the assumption that this covenanted nation is destined to lead the world through a separation from it. This is the negative side of the exemplary construct: the nation should remain distant from the entanglements of the world for the sake of its continuing purity. Washington's farewell address prominently counseled the republic to avoid entangling alliances.[18] A deep strand of isolationism continued to be very powerful through World War II and threatens even today to influence conduct of foreign relations in a complex multipolar world. This strand in the American mythic collective self-understanding is also rooted in an originating impulse at the foundation of colonial life. It and the more positive version are logical constructions of America's conceptualization of national destiny. Exemplary versions of American collective identity are associated with mission. They are conceived in terms of perfecting a society as a demonstration to the world at large.

The other dominant mythic pattern of national mission might be termed emissary. Here the burden borne by the community is to bring other nations to the truth by the action of the faithful American polity. This pattern is as deeply woven into American culture as the exemplary one.[19] If to the first generation New England was to be a "city set on a hill," the same settlers undertook not only to Christianize but also to civilize the indigenous Indian cultures. The point in this context is not to offer retrospective moral judgments about cultural interaction, but to stress how the emissary element in American destiny has been as prominent as the exemplary. American myths about collective purpose have rationalized apparently contradictary social goals: intervention in the affairs of other nations, as well as isolation from them: a war to make the world safe for democracy, as well as an example of democracy held forth to the world; and a crusade against atheistic communism, as well as perfection of the covenanted nation as a god-fearing republic.

No less familiar than the basic mythic *form* of mission is the content of presumed end or purpose of the national covenant. The summary term, democracy, has had broad cultural currency since the early national period. The fullest analysis of this ideal in national life was given by Alexis de Toqueville in his celebrated discussion of the new American culture.[20] But the elements of which it was composed had emerged at least by the eighteenth century. Recent scholarship has explored in great detail two aspects of the democracy that was forming in the Revolutionary epoch. On the one hand, the colonial political leaders worked over several decades to adapt British Whig political culture to the colonies so that liberty and property became watchwords of their emerging cause.[21] On the other hand, the Calvinist-evangelical religious forces secularized the content of the millennial tradition so that achievement of independence and a self-directed republic was the effective content of the anticipated divine Kingdom.[22] Thus an independent political order committed to democracy construed in terms of individual rights to liberty and property *was* the mission of the covenanted nation.

The language of the American political realm has incorporated these values so basically that we do not often reflect upon how innovative they were in the context of the pre-enlightenment European political traditions, which had emphasized the necessity of subjection to authority. To be sure, resistance to tyrants had been discussed in those traditions, and the English had brought down a particular king, although the reign of the line was restored in a decade. But the systematic elaboration of rule by the people as the substance of a nation's high sense of mission and the achievement of a tolerable approximation to that ideal was a signal event in history.

This complex of mythic materials is basic to what we may now recognize as the cultural nationalism of the new republic.[23] These elements are "givens." Conflict does develop in American history over interpretation of them. In particular, the *degree* of union made necessary by the covenant and the implications of the ideals with respect to race led to bloody and bitter civil strife in the 1860s. But the struggle was over *interpretation* of the basic mythic substratum. The cultural nationalism was simply subject to different constructions. This plasticity of the myths is made all the more evident by reflection upon the struggles for civil rights in the 1960s. Conservatives feared the radicalism, thinking it inspired by Communist ideals, or perhaps by third-world struggles. But it was amply evident in the collapse of radical activities that, although a few leaders may have been inspired by other cultural traditions, the recruits to the cause and the consequent power of the movement came from the complex of fundamental American democratic myths.

The content of American cultural nationalism is democracy, and it may assume both exemplary and emmissary forms. The mythic elaboration places this realized and secularized millennium in a broadly historical setting. Thus mythic materials incorporate an explanatory reference to their origin. Turned in this way, the basic theme is one of chosenness. America has been selected for its covenant, or mission. In this respect the form of the myth is also ineradicably Hebraic, for ancient Israel provides the dominant model for a community bearing this burden of historical destiny. It is common knowledge that the founding generation conceived of America as "God's New Israel."[24] The number of sermons in the revolutionary epoch constructed around this mythic identity is remarkable, and their explicitness on this point is striking. The directness of the identification is diminished in the subsequent elaboration of the culture, but allusions and references to America as Israel suffuse even apparently secular materials.[25] While at one level such familiar language as "promised land" and "city set on a hill" are only biblical allusions, the master image, or figure which frames and sets their true content, is the type of Israel as God's chosen people. Thus the apparently secularized expressions have a deeper reasonance which locates the origins of the American mission very precisely even when they are not explicity elaborated.

It would be an error, however, to assume that mythic constructs were directly derived from the Bible, or that, in this case, the myths relating to Israel as "chosen people" were not already elaborated as received. To explore the best example, the image of Israel as a nation chosen of God had already undergone significant adaptation: a basic element in the Puritan construction of an alternative future for England was its election by God as the new Israel.[26] This was most directly developed in John Foxe's *Book of Martyrs,* which had explicitly identified England as God's chosen instrument within the scheme of universal redemption, and it was applied and refined in the trials of the English Civil Wars. [27] So English Puritan mythology stands directly behind and contributes to the forming of the American sense of its origins. In its collective self-understanding, America becomes, so to speak, the third, and presumably last, Israel following England's faithlessness.

If American myths of origin develop this basic tradition of chosenness rooted in Israel's self-understanding, they also synthesize additional figures or images. From the broadly classical tradition associated with Rome, America derived myths of republican ideals and virtues.[28] From this same source came the tradition of political universalism through the heritage of the empire and joined to a strain of salvific universalism from the Christian tradition. So in the mythic construct the mission flows from many origins which, however disjunctive in their sources, have become synthesized into a cultural nationalism centered in the American covenant.

Mythic elaboration of the sense of mission within the culture, including understanding of its origin, is relatively abstract. The powerful hold of these images upon the public comes through their being rendered highly specific. The specificity derives from larger-than-life figures who are believed to have acted in critical ways to create the nation and from particular events in which the mythic material is condensed or focussed. In the dynamics of religious symbolism founding figures are extremely important.[29] The founder creates and establishes the cosmos which provides a framework of general intelligibility for the collectivity. This is especially true in the case of religions in the Hebraic tradition, with their emphasis on history as linear development from a beginning to an end. Moses is the archetype, of course, and remains a human figure of larger-than-life proportions: though he has ascended the holy mountain and communed with God, he is barred from entering the promised land. Major religions deriving from the Hebraic tradition certainly identify founders, among whom Jesus and Muhammad are the best known figures. In important respects, even minor movements within the broader tradition develop self-definitions in terms of the particular originators of their ways. Martin Luther and John Wesley are examples of relatively recent reformers who have been elevated as founders of Christian movements. Since they are readily accessible as persons through rich historical materials, we know of their well-documented ambivalence toward their roles.[30] We must assume no less about all founders, especially those remote in space and time.[31]

Among the outsized historico/mythic figures of American national culture, George Washington is pre-eminent: "First in War, first in peace, first in the hearts of his countrymen." The remarkable consideration is that in the course of his lifetime, Washington had *become* a mythic figure.[32] His achievements as military leader in the struggle for independence cast him as a young Moses leading his people out of captivity. Like Moses, having achieved success in the one role, he pressed on to lead his people to a subsequent goal, a promised land. Interesting questions can be raised about the degree to which Washington's very status as legendary figure transcending petty disputes was itself a major factor in the achievement of a viable new nation. Whatever the estimate of that issue, his role as two-term president who relinquished power voluntarily assured the further elaboration of his mythic stature. In the compounding of the legend, Washington not only served as the American Moses, but as well fulfilled the type represented by Joshua. Indeed, the type of

Jesus as divine-human was not altogether beyond the collective American imagination. The play of mythic imagination easily encompassed his mother, Mary, so inevitably identified with the mother of Jesus. (In this respect Martha, the wife, posed more problems.)

Washington, the Father of his country, is the dominant figure of the mythic national materials. But he is not alone in the pantheon of American national cult figures.[33] Political leaders who have contributed to American national success at turning points in its history have been elevated to this status. Jefferson more clearly than Hamilton or Madison is a legendary figure within the culture. Jackson is far more prominent than others who followed the first generation.[34] Certainly Lincoln, who in his death embraced the ambiguity of coerced union, was thereby transfigured more than Grant, the victorious military leader in civil war.[35] Theodore Roosevelt and Woodrow Wilson represent the American achievement of stature among the nations and are more central to the cult of the national covenant than, shall we say, William Jennings Bryan. Franklin Delano Roosevelt and Dwight D. Eisenhower, for different reasons, more clearly belong to this circle than does Harry S. Truman. In his death John F. Kennedy, like Lincoln, was immediately transfigured, while Lyndon Johnson and Richard Nixon to this point remain outside the cult through defeat and disgrace, respectively.

It is the nature of the presidential office in the American polity for its incumbents to be prime candidates for mythic stature within the national self-understanding. But others can be transfigured to become part of the covenant. Martin Luther King is a fine example in our own time of a leader who created conflict within the social order. Through transcending that conflict in death, however, he became symbol for an enlarged understanding of the national community so that it could embrace as its true ends many of the goals he pursued. The basis for creation of mythic national figures is popular perception that the community is decisively enlarged through his or her contribution. This is certainly why Jackson was the symbol of his age. We should probably view extra-political figures like Edison or Lindberg in this same perspective. Individuals associated with conflict-producing stress within the social fabric can also become part of the national mythos. While in their lifetimes "barons" like John D. Rockefeller and Andrew Carnegie are viewed as threats in a way Edison and the early Lindberg are viewed as benign, they become transformed through philanthropic legacies and historical distance.[36]

The identities of mythic figures derive from the contributions they seem to make to the history of the national community. They move the nation toward the fulfillment of its ostensible mission. In this sense the legendary figures are linked to mythic events even as the national origin is linked to its presumed destiny. In this respect the central event is in the founding of the community. Strictly speaking, from a critical historical perspective, the founding of this nation cannot be highly localized or sharply circumscribed in space and time. Recent work has made it clear that the American war for independence follows a long period of increasing development of colonial society as well as progressive alienation from England in narrowly political terms.[37] Systematic overt opposition appears at least by 1760 and fitfully continues for over one half a century. But in the mythic world, the central events take place in 1776, when resolve is manifested to make a decisive break with England—that is, to declare independence. No matter that it takes a decade and a half to secure the territory and to develop a government at once adequate to political needs and acceptable to the contending colonial sovereignties. A mythic construction of the event works to interpret and condense the significance of large-scale transformations by means of attention to particular changes which come to stand for the whole. This process is similar to the way Washington's achievement in its legendary version—to lead the colonial insurgents to military victory as well as to preside over consolidation of political authority—works to exclude all other claimants. Perhaps a subsequent mythic figure of a scale roughly comparable to Washington could arise only with a new generation celebrating the reorientation of the national community away from the seaboard and embracing with systematic conquest the inner continent. Jackson, then, is the first public figure after Washington to achieve remotely comparable stature. By comparison, Jefferson's achievements lack the focus provided by decisive transformation of the society, however interesting he remains to intellectuals and however attractive to idealists.

Certainly a number of events contribute to the definition of the national community in the ante-bellum period. Defending national integrity against the British in the War of 1812, augmenting the territory of the community through diplomacy, purchase, force, removing indigenous peoples from their lands and clustering them on reservations, incorporating colonizers from other nations as well as increased numbers of immigrants—all are mundane events at one level. Each, however, is transformed as it enters the mythic realm of American collective self-understanding. Each comes to be understood in terms of the national mission and becomes interpreted through the national covenant. All of these events, however, pale before the symbol of the bloody civil struggle. Certainly division over slavery and economic rivalry were the immediate causes of the War between the States. With respect to the national community, however, the struggle became most basically a battle for possession of the covenant.[38] The union was preserved on northern terms, thereby subordinating the South for a century. Slavery was abolished, but by conspiring to assign second-class status to blacks. In this framework, the national covenant is the moral claim that the community continues as elect under divine authorization. So the Civil War sanctified the nation through the terrible blood sacrifice of lives. Thus purified, the nation was prepared for missions which quite literally have reached around the globe.

The Spanish skirmish, entrance into European interstate struggles, a world war on two fronts, and finally the role of leading of the "forces of light" arrayed against those of "darkness" in a Cold War—are all events which took place within the nation's mythic self-understanding and thereby came under the national covenant. Thus, America in the mid-decades of this century had a pathetically sure sense of its destiny. This is the symbolic, or mythic, background to the trauma of war in Southeast Asia. The American nation, in a classical reversal of roles, experienced the frustration of empire in trying to control an indigenous revolution at the periphery of its sphere of influence. The mythic self-understanding of the American collectivity was expressed in the national covenant; the self-serving and self-aggrandizing aspects of that covenant lie starkly revealed in the agony of the Vietnam War.

In this symbol world of mythic constructs the national collectivity is identified through origins and destinies, heroic figures, and significant events. The master image is the covenanted nation. But while the form of that construct and its appearance connote antiquity and constancy, the reality of the national community is forever changing. This means that each generation has collectively "owned the covenant" in a rather different sense than was true of the faithful in colonial Puritan life.[39] Mythic symbolic constructs always represent given social interests and reflect contemporary issues. Therefore the national covenant is continuously undergoing accommodation or revision. It has been malleable and plastic, even fluid, rather than brittle, set, or constrained. In this sense, the covenant has no independence from the national culture—indeed it is perhaps the most distinctive and condensed expression of it.

This substantial cultural legacy of myth about the national community is the fundamental means through which religious understanding has been a continuing part of American public life. These mythic materials illustrate how even American secular collective self-understanding has been freighted with religious significance. In effect, these materials have created and preserved religious identity for the nation. As myth they have located American society in a cosmic framework and have oriented both collective and individual activity within it. This understanding of the nation as a covenanted community has been the basic religious aspect of the culture.

There is a problem, however, arising from this perception of the material: How can it and related data be interpreted with more precision? The data are manifestly religious in form and reference. Further they have a recognized religious function, at least as contemporary social theory has understood religious aspects of societies and cultures. Taken as a whole, however, the substantial mass is largely undifferentiated; it is a relatively shapeless deposit of cultural materials. Without more subtle intellectual discriminations, little more can be claimed than that the materials constitute a set of myths. Their precise religious status and their particular religious functions in the culture are unclear. The material has frequently received attention of course in formal literary terms, and it has been viewed as folk material. It has also been interpreted in historical or genetic frameworks, to suggest several conventional approaches.[40] But no one of these frameworks significantly advances interpretation of the material in more strictly *religious* terms. To achieve this end, the religious aspects of the material must be identified with more precision and appropriate approaches to them must be developed. Lacking this, religious analysis of the data cannot be achieved.

The strategy we adopt in this study will distribute the relevant mythic materials into different sets and analyze more closely their characteristics and contents. To be sure, as the above discussion has made clear, the overall cast of this material is deeply Hebraic, and the content does concern collective origins and destinies, outsized agents, and fateful events. But such general observations and crude attempts at descriptive classification are not sufficient. We must seek to analyze those means through which the mythic material works to generate the identity of the American community. The continuing reaffirmation and redefiniton of the American polity must be the central subject. In this more analytical framework, attention shifts to certain basic locations or expressions of religion, even functions of religion, in a modern society. Four approaches to systematic study of these religio-mythic materials of the covenanted community seem especially promising.

First, religion provides a language of intelligibility about the social world in its least-bounded context. Thus, we will review materials of the public realm for evidence of formally articulated beliefs about this national community as it is distinct from other communities. To advance such a program, however, the search for appropriate evidence must be systematic. Our search for beliefs about the national community will be limited to presidential state papers, and we will insist upon review of comparable data from all incumbents. This makes it all possible to look for patterns (if such exist) in the systematic public use of religious language and to estimate the continuities and discontinuities (if they exist) in the religious references. Our formal question thus becomes: Has a set of beliefs about America been articulated by the American presidents in a way that bestows religious intelligibility upon the national community?

A parallel kind of inquiry concerns patterned behavior as a means to achieve collective identity. Is public behavior in American society systematically constrained in ways that, parallel to the articulation of beliefs on behalf of the whole society by the president, a comparable delineation of the collectivity is achieved? Are there ritual aspects to American social and political life that center on the definition of the polity as the structure of the community? Are these aspects sharply differentiated from the patterns of behavior which are more widely diffused throughout the society? This is a counterpart to the systematic inquiry into patterns of formally articulated belief and is important as a complementary means to analyze the mythic materials. On the hypothesis that there is an American public religion, it must be understood as defining patterns of behavior and constraining actions even as, through establishing a horizon of general belief, it identifies that realm of behavior which is American culture.

Beyond the distinction between behavior and belief as a means of analyzing in religious terms the mythic substratum of American collective life, two additional approaches may be employed. As any viable community exists through time, it provides meaning by giving coherence to the lives of individuals and groups within it. Collective beliefs set out a community's convictions about itself in relation to other communities, or as it faces outward. Meanings indicate how a community is experienced by those within it, or how it feels from the inside. The operative question thus becomes: Are there recurrent images through which Americans have explained individual experiences and found their group identities *within* the American community?

Finally, at least in thoroughly differentiated societies with complex institutions, religions achieve organizational expression or they depend upon social structures. Without an institutional fabric to sustain patterns of belief and behavior and to communicate meanings, individuals and groups lose social orientation and finally undergo disorganization. Thus, the place of social institutions in the transmission of religio-mythic materials becomes a critical consideration in refining the analysis of public religion in America.

These four special topics flow from the recognition that religious aspects of American collective life are manifested in rich cultural materials. The topics represent the respective subjects for the next chapters. In turn, each chapter will push forward the analysis of public religion under one aspect, or formal category. Each study represents a critical review in a restricted analytical framework of basic historical materials associated with the national covenant. In one sense each of these inquiries can stand by itself. But in another sense each requires the others to bound the circle of analysis. The outcome intended is informed religious criticism of public religion in

America. A thesis implicit in the discussion, and increasingly the burden of the whole, is that theoretical clarity is prerequisite to informed discussion of American public religion. The concluding chapter turns explicitly to that issue, distinguishing various models which stand as major options in the interpretation of the national covenant, or the materials of American public religion.

Chapter 3

THE RELIGIOUS LANGUAGE
OF AMERICAN PRESIDENTS

In beginning his first inaugural address (in 1953) with a three-paragraph prayer addressed to "Almighty God," Dwight D. Eisenhower provided a *locus classicus* for analysis of the religious content of formal presidential language.[1] It was an unquestioned conviction of this modern soldier-statesman that the American nation was founded on a belief in God, and that this religious foundation had supported the republic throughout episodic trials and periods of triumph. His oft-reported comment, frequently the subject of scorn or ridicule among intellectuals, that "America was founded on a belief in God—and I don't care what it is," should be taken as a serious testimony to the depth of his belief.[2] Ike simply assumed that the realm of common life is grounded in a public religion. Eisenhower's straightforward belief and his forthright avowal of it is unusual; most presidents have been relatively guarded in their religious references. As politicians who have survived the hazards of repeated public exposure they instinctively have known that while religious modes of address may build political support and consensus they may as often prove to be divisive.

Why is religious language in the public realm so problematical in America? At least two kinds of answers to this question must be juxtaposed: one has to do with the *nature* of religious language; the other concerns the particular place of religion in American society.

It is generally recognized, thanks to the insights of Emile Durkheim, that religious language is connected at a very deep level with the reality of social groups.[3] Of course in the most obvious sense, languages are social conventions, means of rendering experience intelligible to individuals in terms of their collective associations. According to this definition, all languages are identified with, in some sense make possible, communities of whatever scale. But religious language is of a special sort because it is concerned with particular kinds of questions, especially those having to do with the horizon or symbolic framework of social life. Different religious symbol systems establish the horizons in different ways. Some symbol systems are given a historical cast, and the religions which make use of them are deeply concerned with questions of origins, identities, destinies. The preceding chapter has already called attention to relevant mythic material of this kind in American culture. Other religious symbol systems are more metaphysical, grounding the associated cultures in metaphors drawn from nature. Of course complex religious symbol systems often combine these kinds of imagery. But whatever the special tone or the particular mode of the horizon, it serves to mark out a realm of intelligibility within which a cultural system can be sustained. Therefore, it is necessary for a culture that religious issues be addressed—if only implicitly. And it inheres in the religious use of language that its references have broad scope, pointing to the most general assumptions and conditions of cultural existence. This function is of the essence of religious language. In that sense, what we know about the function of religious language in societies and their cultures indicate that religion is necessarily associated with the public realm.

At the same time, the United States has been extraordinarily pluralistic in harboring a variety of social groups and religious identities. Large numbers of the groups have been transplanted cuttings from European, African, and Asian societies.[4] But that image finally fails. The process of migration has worked a transformation upon each ethnic group so that the identity in the new world is changed from what it was in the old. In large part because of the religious freedom offered in the American republic, the identities of the ethnic groups so transplanted to America have been expressed in religious terms. No less have indigenous groups frequently expressed their identities in religious terms—for many of the same reasons. The dynamics of American society have, if you will, made the realm of religious symbols and language a primary means of establishing differentiation and claiming uniqueness, albeit in a way not threatening to national unity. Empirically speaking, not only is the United States extraordinary among the modernized societies of the world in the *degree* of religious activity and affiliation within it, it is also extraordinary in the *number* of different religions which are vital within it.[5]

Religious language is problematical in the American public realm because contradictory impulses are at work. On the one side, the culture is religiously plural in the extreme; on the other, the society as a whole, like every other society, requires, especially in times of stress and crisis, the self-definition which is provided through religiously-used language. These tensions go very deep and suggest why the subject of this chapter is so elusive. Religious language of the public realm is veiled, obscure, and shifting. How can it be analyzed?

In proposing that there was a civil religion in America, Robert Bellah advanced as primary evidence for his case the addresses given by American presidents on the occasions of their inaugurations. As much as one quarter of his original article was an analysis and exegesis of the address given by John F. Kennedy on January 20, 1961. He characterized the speech in the following passage.

The whole address can be understood as only the most recent statement of a theme that lies very deep in the American tradition, namely the obligation, both collective and individual, to carry out God's will on earth. This was the motivating spirit of those who founded America, and it has been present in every generation since. Just below the surface throughout Kennedy's inaugural address, it becomes explicit in the closing statement that God's work must be our own.[6]

For Bellah, Kennedy's address stood in the tradition of inaugural declarations by presidents on assumption of the office. He thought that when properly interpreted, this tradition constituted important evidence for both the reality and also the shape of American civil religion. This assumption has continued to be important for Bellah and others in discussions of civil religion.[7]

In searching for the religious use of language in the public realm which might be evidence for public religion, one might sensibly begin with a review of the formal addresses in which the presidents have understood themselves to speak for, and sometimes to, all the people. The inaugural address is such an event; so too is the annual State of the Union message. These are routine occasions on which the incumbent might be expected to make references to the public religion within the culture, since each concerns beginnings (of a new administration, of a new year) and each directs attention to desired outcomes (such as a renewed nation). Further, we might look to critical episodes in the culture, such as the death in office of an incumbent president, or the searching reflection necessitated by civil struggle or international strife, to occasion further disclosure of religious assumptions operating in the public realm. Within this framework, the issue will turn out to be not *whether* there are references in the political culture which have religious aspects, but what *interpretation* should be given to them. Among the obvious options are the following: (1) Are they evidence for a coherent religious tradition centered in the public realm, as in the civil religion proposal? (2) Are they expressions of a culturally given public religion (republican protestantism, general Christianity, the Judeao-Christian tradition, The American Way of Life)? (3) Are they evidence for personal religious commitments of the incumbent, testifying to his own religious appropriation of the collective event? (4) Are they some combination of the above, possibly in different proportions depending upon the individual and the time?

The inauguration is a ceremony of transition which legitimizes the transfer of power. The addresses of the founding fathers include numerous references to a deity, references which directly reflect eighteenth-century religious formulations. Washington's first address, as an example, referred to "Almighty Being," "Great Author," "Invisible Hand," and "Parent of the human Race."[8] Adams, Jefferson, Madison, and Monroe all followed the practice, each choosing his own specific terms.[9] Generally, the references seem to have reflected the religious usages of the enlightenment-derived religious sub-culture which influenced the Virginians so deeply (as well as Adams to some degree), rather than echoing, for example, the evangelical tone stridently reasserted in the "second great awakening" which was proving to have increasingly wide currency in the society. With the second Adams, slightly more specific and somewhat more traditionally Christian formulations entered the record with his mention of the "Lord" and an invocation of the "Presence of Heaven."[10] From Jackson to Buchanan, references were made by all presidents—"Providence" being the most widely used term, although other more personal formulations were not excluded.[11] It is a relatively straightforward judgment that as civil war loomed the religious allusions became more pronounced. Near the end of his first inaugural, Lincoln made explicitly Christian references.[12] Only with his second and very brief inaugural address, however, did an essentially religious formulation move from the periphery to the center of an inaugural address. The sophisticated and explicit theological reflections within Lincoln's second inaugural mark it as categorically unique in the attempt it represents to explicate a religious framework of national destiny.[13] Kennedy's is the only one to approach it in its level of subtlety in formulating manifestly religious issues.

After Lincoln, all presidents, with McKinley the most notable,[14] included passing and relatively conventional references to the divine. But this evidence certainly does not argue for a differentiated civic cult. At the most it suggests that various incumbents felt constrained to make reference to the limits of the culture and its dependence on transcendent sources. This pattern was broken not, as might be thought, by Woodrow Wilson, but by Warren G. Harding in his 1921 address.[15] From Harding through the beginning of Franklin D. Roosevelt's third term (1941), the allusions were very general and, at least to a careful reading in the present, thoroughly conventional in content.[16]

The coming of World War II apparently led the second

Roosevelt to introduce references suggesting a more active conception of the role that the divine might play in
American life. This is an interesting parallel to the markedly increased intensity of religious references between
Lincoln's first and second addresses. Roosevelt concluded
his third inaugural, on the spirit of American life and the
destiny of the nation, with a direct invocation of divine
direction of national life: "As Americans, we go forward, in
the service of our country, by the Will of God."[17] He thus
began, we may see in retrospect, a period which waned
with the Kennedy inaugural.[18] In its course, there was
regular and direct invocation of divine agency as source,
power, and protector of the American nation in its international struggle against atheistic communism. In 1949,
Truman characterized the differences between the powers
of light and darkness, concluding his speech with the
assurance that ". . . with God's help, the future of man-
kind will be assured in a world of justice, harmony, and
peace."[19] Eisenhower began his 1953 address with the
prayer to which reference has been made. By implication, if
not in content, this prayer carried on the dualistic conceptions, introduced by Roosevelt and developed by Truman.[20] Eisenhower struck much the same note in his
second inaugural address four years later.[21]

It is most important to recognize the virtually Manichaean religious tone of these modern religious conceptions articulated in the public realm by American presidents. This period was the immediate background to John
F. Kennedy's address, and judicious interpretation of the
latter requires that it be placed in this setting. Robert
Bellah, of course, made much of the three references
Kennedy included. In this sense, the address may be read as
comparable to those which preceded it in terms of the
attention given to religious questions. (Of course, the

whole period between 1940 and 1962 appears to be somewhat anomalous when placed against the general pattern
of addresses.) What marks it off from the others is its
apparent intent.[22] Close reading indicates a careful formulation designed at once to make reference to an ultimate
role of the divine in history, while also bringing to an end a
too-easy identification of proximate American purposes
with ultimate divine intentions. In fact, Kennedy turned
around the formulation which the preceding addresses
implicitly embodied. He was bold enough to suggest that
the will of God might be the proper standard against which
American actions should be judged.[23] In this perspective,
we might conclude that Kennedy self-consciously sought
to terminate what had been a period of rather extraordinary and uncritical identification of American actions
with divine intentions. In any case, this particular address
is the only one other than Lincoln's second which gives
credible evidence of Biblical and general theological lit-
eracy in the formulation of the relationship between national purposes and religious presuppositions. References
in the succeeding addresses by Lyndon B. Johnson, Richard
Nixon, and Jimmy Carter represent a return to the more
conventional formulations noted above. These references
are more readily interpreted as reflections of broader
cultural attitudes refracted through the experience of an
individual than as direct statements which might reflect a
positive civic faith.

It would be foolish to expect (and Bellah certainly did
not) that on the basis of inaugural addresses alone it would
be possible to delineate adequately national religious presuppositions, or public religion, if such may be thought to
exist. At best, we might propose that in them there would
be articulated in oblique ways a sense of national dependence upon transcendent power. It is not surprising that

early nineteenth-century addresses utilized a new-world modification of the religious language of the eighteenth century. Nor is it unexpected that the advent of "political presidents" was reflected in more conventional and popular references to the deity. In America's coming of age in the mid-twentieth century, one might have predicted self-righteous religious conceptions. Finally, presidents who lacked majority support in a divided country, speaking at turning points in the nation's history, might be expected to have insight into the ambiguity of religious claims about the nation, especially if they are viewed in relationship to the tradition of theologically informed reflection on the subject. The inaugural addresses, then, do not provide sufficient material to generalize adequately about religious language in the public realm and certainly not evidence of a type which would permit us to reach an unequivocal conclusion (either way) about a civic faith. Is it possible to advance our analysis on the basis of other kinds of presidential materials?

Let us turn first to the annual message, or the assessment of national health, commonly known as the State of the Union address. Circumstances surrounding delivery of State of the Union addresses have varied through the years, but they do represent a potentially valuable source of evidence for this discussion. While formally addressed to Congress, the annual messages are given to these bodies in their representative capacity only, and few addresses have not been figuratively directed over the heads of the office-holders to their constituents. Especially in times of national trial or when the urgency of social change is felt, we might expect that there would be at least implicit references to a frame or horizon of expectations which would be closely allied with the attempt to forge a national consensus, if not to recite a national credo. Some years ago,

Seymour Fersh systematically analyzed 170 annual messages produced by the 33 incumbents up to 1961.[24] He separated the addresses into several distinct periods and noted within each, among other things, characteristic religious references. In the addresses before the era of Jackson, for example, Fersh found "almost perennial lavish religious thanksgiving."[25] From Jackson on, he discovered that some religious references continued, especially the attribution of growth, health, and peace to divine providence. Characteristically, paragraphs devoted to these subjects were located either at the beginning or near the end of the annual messages. (This coincides with the observation that public religion should constitute a frame for American life.)

Fersh reports that under Lincoln the religious element or strain was continued, but "without the florid embellishment that characterized an earlier generation's writing."[26] It is interesting that Lincoln should have been sparing in the use of such references in his annual messages in view of his profound religious musings and his readiness to introduce explicit religious themes and materials on specific occasions, most notably in his second inaugural address.

From Grant to the middle of the 1880s, a steady decline took place in the number, and a marked lessening in the specificity, of religious phrases in the annual messages.[27] In general, this secularizing trend continued until the time of Franklin D. Roosevelt. One prominent exception was McKinley, who made frequent and full mention of God, superintending providence, and other religious concepts.[28] Although Woodrow Wilson, on whose part conventional religious references might have been expected, made more than his immediate predecessors or successors, the degree of incidence was not high, nor was the elaboration extensive.[29]

With Franklin D. Roosevelt, religious references were again introduced with regularity. They were also characterized by general urbanity.[30] Truman freely included theological considerations in his messages, the tone of them being rather more evangelical than his predecessor's.[31] In his messages Eisenhower continued Truman's essentially dualistic perspective, a religious construction of the world already noted in discussion of the inaugural addresses. They essentially rang changes on the opposition between "God-fearing people" and communist imperialists.[32] As might be expected, Kennedy's religious references were discriminating, undoubtedly calculated with care at once to continue the practice of making direct religious references (a practice cultivated by his predecessors), while at the same time to separate these references from immediate and potentially divisive issues in the politics of the period. More than any other incumbent, he seems to have couched his religious references in terms calculated not to offend the intellectuals who supported him. With Johnson, Nixon, and Carter, the references have continued without a full return to the prominent and frequent invocation of God and providence in relation to national purposes which came so easily to Truman and Eisenhower.

This cursory review of the annual messages and the inaugural addresses does suggest that occupants of the presidential office experience some constraints, at least on certain formal occasions, to introduce manifestly religious references as they interpret national life. While personal, indeed idiosyncratic, notes certainly appear in these materials, the annual message is sufficiently stylized and routinized in important respects so that, as in the case of the inaugural address, the president speaks in a manner required by the office. It would not seem, however, that this has amounted to an ultimate religious framework or horizon in terms of which national life could be consistently interpreted. It is significant that the readiness to make direct religious references connected with social purposes has depended to some degree upon perception of a national crisis. In the early and tentative years of the republic, the religious framework appeared almost as a kind of scaffolding for the new experiment. Thereafter, its significance appears to have declined throughout the century, except for the period in which the nation was put to trial by the experience of internal, or civil, war. With the nation thrust into the international struggle of World War I, a framework again appeared. The experience of international depression and subsequent global war, which became conceived in virtually Manichaean terms, was occasion for sustained development of this framework. The easing of the Cold War and the recognition of a multi-centered as opposed to a bipolar world seems to have been reflected in decreased emphasis upon the direct presentation of religious assumptions as they might relate to the public realm.

In this review of formal presidential language about religion in the public realm, we have not discovered any elaborated and fully articulated intellectual construct of a national faith. We may also conclude that there is pronounced periodicity in the religious references made by incumbents. These seem to have been closely correlated with perceived threats to the society. Religious language about the public realm is occasioned by national crisis.

Perhaps there are other kinds of linguistic materials that would take us closer to the construction given to religion in the public realm. Possibly the most promising direction of inquiry is to review the annual tradition of Thanksgiving proclamations which issue from the Oval Office. For purposes of our analysis in this chapter, the important consideration is the language of the proclamation, rather than the particulars of the holiday itself. Annual proclamations have been routinely issued for some one hundred years. Thus both the form and the content have become highly stylized. As far as I can determine, the modern tradition began with President Grant, and most of the marks of later proclamations were present in his first one.[33]

On October 5, 1869, Grant proposed that Thursday, November 18th "be observed as a day of thanksgiving and of praise and prayer to Almighty God." He recommended assembling in "accustomed places of public worship," there "to unite in the homage and praise due to the bountiful Father of All Mercies and in fervent prayer for the continuance of the manifold blessings he has vouchsafed to us as a people."[34] The logic requiring this action and the grounds leading to it might be summarized in the following elements which are implied if not directly stated:

1. The periodicity of the seasons, especially in the context of the plentitude of the harvest time, "should remind the people of the divine Goodness to the nation."
2. A catalogue of mercies and blessings includes not only the productivity of the land, but good health, a strong economy, social order, and general political stability—international as well as domestic.
3. Formal and collective acknowledgment of the same is appropriate, and such ritual behavior may be efficacious in securing continuation of the divine blessings.
4. Therefore, a particular day should be sanctified by the whole people, though each religious group within the whole should do so in its own fashion.[35]

This formulation, which continues as the basic structure

of the occasion to the present day, was so immediately secure that it was not called into question by national experience to the contrary. At the end of October, 1874, for example, Grant proclaimed November 26th of that year as Thanksgiving Day, and the text issued was virtually interchangeable with the one offered five years previously.[36] It may be significant that Grant did not make religious references in the context of his subsequent annual message, for in previous and less trying years he had lost no opportunity to detail gratitude to "Wise Providence" or "the Giver of all Good."[37] As we shall see, the logic of the antecedent framework, abandoned in the modern Thanksgiving celebrations, would have placed a particular construction upon the experience of economic collapse.

A full analysis of Thanksgiving proclamations might prove to be a promising project under other circumstances. In the present context, however, certain observations are especially pertinent: (1) Far more than in the religious references identified in the inaugural addresses, and also to a greater degree than in the annual messages, the proclamations display continuity of both form and symbols and seem to be evidence for the continuing identity of an ideological structure through time; (2) the setting apart of a day as the year closes in which collective thanksgiving shall be given for blessings experienced by the nation is the core of the tradition; (3) some holders of office embellish that core in the proclamation issued each year. For example, the 1972 proclamation included an extraordinary number of accretions. Direct mention of the early settlers in the New World had been a frequent addition to the basic structure through the years. In this case, President Nixon also included inter-faith references and national allusions (both historical and contemporary), holding up a collage of examples for the nation as it prepared to enter upon collective thanksgiving: Moses at the Red Sea, Jesus preparing to feed the multitudes, Washington at Valley Forge, and the prayer made by an astronaut while on extended flight in space. In spite of the accretions, however, the basic structure which we have already identified stands out as the fundamental model.[38] In other years, at the hands of different presidents, the same materials have been elaborated and reworked in various ways. Benjamin Harrison, to cite one instance, made only brief and passing reference to the blessings of the year (1890), while discoursing at some length on the appropriate means of observing the day, including an oft-used exhortation to practice charity towards the poor.[39] Some of the more loquacious presidents have made of the proclamation an annual message seemingly addressed to the Almighty on the state of the nation. (See as fine examples of this Woodrow Wilson's 1914 message and that of Calvin Coolidge in 1924.[40])

In the annual Thanksgiving proclamations, therefore, there is an important deposit of presidential interpretation of the religious framework of national life. The fundamental unchangingness of formulation in these proclamations that we have discovered, however variously elaborated, may be important evidence that this linguistic tradition certainly has a ceremonial basis. This consideration may have important implications in establishing Thanksgiving as a ritual associated with public religion in America. The characteristics of this tradition, while signifying different things, do signal the possibility that we have identified a body of protean national beliefs that might be construed to represent a framework of national identity, a fundamental religious commitment of the society. On this hypothesis the basic set of values, or the creed, would incorporate the following elements: "American society is dependent on a God whose providence created and sustains the collective life. Corporate and public thanksgiving is the appropriate acknowledgment of that dependent relationship." Certainly nothing in the inaugural and State of the Union materials reviewed above would contradict this formulation; indeed, numerous aspects of various addresses may be interpreted as refractions of such a creed.

If such a public belief structure is present in American society, we should not be surprised that it appears as a severely truncated version of Calvinism. Indeed it seems to be derived from an older covenantal formulation of the proper relationship between nation and deity, perhaps originally Hebraic and more recently Puritan. Of course a developed covenantal elaboration of this religious relationship would specify the conditions and the degree of dependence on the divine will, attribute particular events (catastrophes and crises) to divine displeasure, and trace prosperity and peace to divine benevolence. The logic of the covenantal formulation would also prescribe collective acts of piety—for example, occasional days of humiliation and thanksgiving—as a means of sustaining and renewing the covenant relationship.

It comes as no surprise, then, to discover that a fully elaborated covenantal scheme seems to have had currency in the early republic, falling into disuse from Jackson to Buchanan and being revitalized by Lincoln. The routine of annual Thanksgivings inaugurated by Grant displaced this pattern altogether.[41] This explains why a ceremonial occasion such as Grant proposed to introduce should have been so readily adopted and proved to be so secure. It was an abridgment and consolidation of a more elaborate, if atrophied, tradition. Within the history of the nation, the explicitly covenantal pattern may be traced to the first six months of Washington's initial term, when a day of public thanksgiving and prayer was held on November 26, 1789. This day was set aside not primarily to express gratitude for a bountiful harvest or for prosperity, but rather for two different purposes: (1) to express thanksgiving for the creation of the nation, an achievement which was ascribed to the "Almighty God"; and (2) to offer praise and to make supplication to the deity for continuance of divine benevolence.[42] A national day of thanksgiving in 1795 utilized much the same formulation.[43]

The ritual of collective thanksgiving had been perfected to a fine art by the Puritans in the English civil wars of the seventeenth century. The pattern probably was derived from prior Dutch practice. Brought over into colonial life, it had proved to be a mighty engine in the struggle for independence. The two collective exercises under Washington were technically thanksgivings for mercies already received. In 1798, John Adams proclaimed a day of humiliation (May 9) to "satisfy" divine displeasure; he thus made it plain that the theological acuity of the colonists had not been entirely lost.[44] The same formulation appeared again within the year.[45]

Jefferson, in spite of urgings by associates, did not choose to make use of either the humiliation or the thanksgiving pattern, but James Madison did in the course of the struggle in 1812.[46] A second humiliation was held in September, 1813, and yet a third in January, 1815.[47] Finally, with the achievement of peace and on the advice of the houses of Congress, Madison proclaimed a day of thanksgiving and devout acknowledgment to Almighty God for "His great goodness manifested in the restoring to them the blessings of peace."[48]

These patterns of national repentance and thanksgiving seem not to have been utilized again until the dark days of the War between the States. At that time, Lincoln proclaimed at least three such exercises of national humiliation, but even more often he utilized the instrument of thanksgiving.[49] Indeed, as the union cause seemed to triumph, the thanksgivings he proposed probably presaged the pattern of annual thanksgiving days inaugurated under Grant. (Clearly, Lincoln's particular use of the instruments of national humiliation and thanksgiving had been an attenuation of the original pattern. Madison's utilization of them had entailed a sharper and more classical formulation.) Very little of the underlying covenant premises remained when Woodrow Wilson proclaimed the first Sunday in October, 1914, as a "Special Day for Prayer and Supplication"[50] (repeated in 1917), or when he declared May 30, 1918, a "day of public humiliation, prayer, and fasting."[51]

A conventional explanation for the devolution of religious beliefs from the covenant-based premises of the humiliation-thanksgiving pattern to the now more than century-old Thanksgiving Day celebrations would be that it manifested a secularization of the society. This is to beg the question of how secularization is to be defined—a difficult topic. (I intend a descriptive usage for purposes of broadly characterizing changed patterns of social life and do not mean to imply a necessarily evolutionary framework, certainly not one of inevitable stages.) Without excluding this interpretation, however, a complementary explanation would be that the absence of a crisis threatening the continuation of the federal union has meant that it has not been necessary or urgent to articulate a refined and exact covenantal formulation of public faith. Other than in the first years of the nation, the War of 1812, and the War between the States, the future of the union has not been so in doubt for prolonged periods as to require elaborately rationalized and stylized collective behavior, including self-referential religious explanation, visibly to display the substance of the union.

In the crisis of extraordinary presidential succession there has been, of course, the possibility of widespread doubt about the preservation of the national union. It is interesting to take note of the way in which threats to the office of the presidency have prompted reaffirmation in linguistic form of something like the basic creed of the Thanksgiving Day tradition. With the death of Harrison, for example, Tyler moved to make May 14, 1841, a day of fasting and prayer.[52] So too at the death of Lincoln, Johnson set aside "a special period for again humbling ourselves before Almighty God, in order that the bereavement [which was also authorized by official action of the new President], should be sanctified to the nation."[53] Having committed the initial indiscretion of setting this exercise for a Sunday, traditionally a day of Christian rejoicing, President Johnson hastily made amends by moving it to a Thursday (June 1, 1865).[54] Chester Arthur made September 26, 1881, a day of "sorrowful submission to the will of Almighty God" upon the death of President Garfield.[55] So too, McKinley's death occasioned a day of mourning and prayer conjoined to his burial (September 19, 1901). The note of formal humiliation was missing in the proclamation issued by Roosevelt, but not the requirement of "submission to the will of Almighty God."[56] Virtually the same arrangements in the same language were made by Calvin Coolidge, who reserved August 10, 1923, for national mourning at the death of Harding.[57] Within the experience of many of us, the assassination of President Kennedy led to the National Day of Mourning on November 23, 1963.[58]

In reflecting upon the assassination of President Kennedy as an event in the national life, Sidney Verba posed an important question:

> What holds a complicated and pluralistic political society like the United States together? We used to think it was a common democratic ideology, but lately we are not so sure. Americans apparently do not think in terms of politics in any but the vaguest terms; the commitment to democratic values does not appear to extend much below the level of slogans.

From this observation, Verba moved on to a superficially contradictory conclusion:

> But this may not mean that common beliefs are irrelevant to the political system. What the Kenkedy assassination may show is that the level of commitment to politics is both more intense than that revealed by the usual public-opinion-surveying techniques and that the commitment is not closely related to any particular political ideology, issue or controversy. . . ; and it is a commitment that lies beneath the surface of ordinary day-to-day politics. As such, it may be a kind of primordial emotional attachment that is necessary for the long-term maintenance of a political system. It is not the rather fragile support that is based solely on a calculation of interests; it is support based on a longer-run, less rational sort of commitment.[59]

In effect, Verba's reflections amount to support for the judgment that the kind of phenomena reviewed in this chapter is clear evidence for the relatively well-established, but infrequent, use of religious formulations with respect to the public realm.

But to say this much begs exceedingly important questions about how the evidence should be put to use. One kind of question concerns the *extent* of relevant data. To give coherence to this particular inquiry, we have reviewed a relatively narrow body of material regularly issued as part of the conduct of the presidential office: the inaugural addresses, the State of the Union messages, and the Thanksgiving proclamations. There is a vast array of pronouncements, messages, speeches, letters, and memoranda associated with that office, all of which is to be viewed as potential linguistic evidence for religious constructions of the public realm. Unsystematic sampling of this material has convinced me that the yield of relevant data would be so slight that further research along these lines would probably not be markedly productive. Procedurally, it is critical to undertake exhaustive review of any given class of material. Only selective review of occasional documents—for example, a particular letter or certain speeches (without reference to all possibly relevant letters or possibly relevant speeches)—would fundamentally qualify any serious claims made on the basis of the evidence so discovered.

Beyond the strictly presidential materials, additional evidence multiplies in dizzying fashion: formal Congressional materials, legal struggles (however resolved at whatever levels), materials of state governors, the records of legislatures. Theoretically, all records relating to the conduct of government are potential locations in which to discover religious language in the public realm. Furthermore, beyond such governmental materials, we might expect to find data originating from journalists, preachers, poets, and public-spirited citizens. With greater or less directness, these materials might either analyze the national polity in religious terms, or use religious language about it. Many fine studies exist which have highlighted particular points of view or certain relevant attitudes in such data.[60] Again, the issue of selectivity in relationship to responsible use of data must be taken into account.

An altogether different kind of question concerns the appropriate approach to be adopted to interpret the relevant evidence. In particular, what *kind* of model of religion seems appropriate for interpretation of the data? The presidential addresses, as an example, do not seem to provide evidence that a highly structured religion centers in the public realm. Nor do the Thanksgiving Day materials seem to be evidence for a ritualistic kind of religion. These issues will remain as we explore other kinds of evidence that the American polity has associated with it piety of a particular kind. What the linguistic evidence does suggest is that the inquiry is worth pursuing.

Chapter 4

RITUALISTIC BEHAVIOR OF AMERICAN PUBLIC LIFE

We commonly assume that American social life does not embody the various, richly textured cultural patterns conventionally attributed to more ancient societies. American intellectuals have repeatedly looked to Europe as the fount of culture. From time to time, later generations have sought wisdom in the east. In the nineteenth century, the European trip was considered the capstone to learning and became one experience held in common by the children of successful business families. In addition, generations of American authors and artists have often chosen to live abroad, realizing creative impulses and discovering comradeship in turning away from aspects of American society they have considered oppressive. Finally, in the last quarter century, the value of a trip to Europe has been taken for granted in widely differing circles. Underlying these specific patterns has been a common attitude that in the absence of a recognized high culture in America little culture worthy of attention can be said to exist.[1]

A perspective which emphasizes the deficiencies of high culture in the United States is widely accepted in the society. It is a point of view seemingly confirmed by the brilliant and variegated contributions made by that generation of European emigrees forced to seek refuge in this nation in the course of the 1930s and 1940s.[2] It also represents a systematic bias, especially on the part of intellectuals, against serious interest in the indigenous culture, even when that medium sustains them. While from the perspective of an anthropologist or an historian such a judgment is analytically unsupportable, its influence must be recognized.[3] If high culture in America is thought to be deficient, however, or if ceremonial aspects of American life seem superficial or even gauche, it simply does not follow that there is not a distinctive culture present in the society. In short, a low estimate of the high culture of the United States, which has sometimes amounted to little more than a collective inferiority complex, ought not to prejudice serious study of those patterns of behavior and action which suffuse American social life and make it distinctive and identifiable.

Of course, there have been numerous attempts in recent decades to delineate the "American national character," a concept related in significant ways to this issue. Some studies have been purely descriptive, others have been informed by psychological or sociological theories. Certainly both kinds are relevant to an analysis of civil society in terms of a culture of operative values. The present study will not attempt to review that literature in detail, for it is vast and diffuse. Nor will it argue for the validity or significance of one or another particular approach to the issues which underlie it (especially as one might exclude others). In many ways, Will Herberg's analysis of the American Way of Life and subsequent discussions of the issues do that sufficiently well to illustrate the strengths and limitations of such an approach to the American national character. In this chapter we intend to push ahead into an analysis of the patterns of interaction within American political and social life. This should illuminate ritual aspects of collective behavior relevant to the issue of piety, or religious practice, which appears to be directed toward the American polity. This is to inquire further into the problematic succinctly identified by Sidney Verba as the "primordial emotional attachment that is necessary for the long-term maintenance of a political system."[4]

One implication of Verba's fundamental point is that systematic consideration should be given to additional kinds of phenomena. That "longer-run, less rational sort of attachment" to a political system[5] that he postulated would more likely be manifested in persistent patterns of behavior than in declarations by presidents of the United States or in their codified proclamations. Journalistic observers, as well as ordinary citizens, are not slow to recognize that there are patterns of behavioral response in American life which constitute a widely if not universally accepted social language. These are not so much values, in a conventional sense, as patterns of expectation of behavior under different kinds of conditions. Since they control interaction within society, these patterns provide us with an identifiable culture in the analytic sense, if not in a high or self-consciously artistic sense. This realm of social behavior is surely expressed through political life, but it also extends well beyond it. Are there in this realm, we might ask, distinctively *American* patterns of interaction? If so, they may be viewed as a kind of evidence for an American piety toward the nation parallel in important respects to the linguistic materials analyzed in the last chapter (admittedly, the tip of an iceberg, since we reviewed only those formally associated with the office of president).

At least one reason for the recent interest in civil religion in American society has been the manner in which this concept identifies, organizes perception of, and finally suggests an explanation for a range of patterned observances in the culture. The hold of such ritual patterns upon

Americans is reflected in the degree to which they are routines at or below the threshold of individual consciousness. They have become so natural as not to require elaborate legends of origin and significance. Most are simply taken for granted in the common life; about a few, there is only a marginal self-consciousness. Full recognition of them comes, if at all, out of the experience of immersion in another culture, or on the basis of the tutoring we receive at the feet of foreign observers. (It is not at all accidental that Robert Bellah, who effectively set out the concept of civil religion, should have been a student of Japanese and other Asian societies.[6] His heightened sensitivity to the distinctive forms and patterns of American life derives in part from the analytic perspective developed in his systematic study of other cultures. Having studied the role of religion in Tokugawa society, he turned logically to the application of his insight to the American case.)

In searching for behavioral patterns in American culture, we are faced at the outset with a special problem: ethnographic materials about the American cultural past are much less readily available than the linguistic materials reviewed in the preceding chapter. It is a part of our culture that we have relatively complete access, for example, to the formal messages delivered by the United States presidents. Concurrently, much less adequate descriptions of behavioral patterns of American life remain. A partial explanation probably lies in the protestant orientation of our culture toward words. Another part is that familiar, or normative, behavior seems not to require observation, whereas the unusual or the deviant is worthy of notice. In this sense, there is probably better ethnographic material about the American Indian cultures than there is about the culture(s) which displaced them. Similarly, because they were different and unusual, the classical "first areas of settlement" through which generations of immigrants passed were more adequately described than succeeding areas. The patterns of assimilation adopted by the second and subsequent generations to achieve full entrance into the society did not challenge American ways so deeply.

At least in principle, there ought to be a remedy for this in the writings produced by those Europeans curious about things American. Of course a considerable literature was produced by visitors. Some of it was intended to have a very practical result: to provide guidance to prospective immigrants. Much more was offered to entertain interested readers with America's wonders and/or foibles. Within this literature, it is interesting and probably significant that much of the reporting for the English-speaking peoples exhibits a tone-deafness with respect to ceremonial or ritual religious and political behavioral patterns. At least a part of this is due to the rationalist cast of English religious and political life, especially among the middle and upper classes. Without the experience of frequent alternations in governments (which threatened continental nations) or subjection to prolonged church-state struggles (in which competing claims were made for the loyalties of citizens through symbolic and ceremonial means), the British observers were simply less struck by the question of how and whether the American nation was developing patterns of behavior which amounted to, in our terms, a distinctive culture with a powerful hold on members of the society.

There is more sensitivity to these issues, it seems, among the French observers, although generally less attention has been paid to these aspects of their reports than to some others. For example, Toqueville's comments about American religion in Volume I of his study, especially his

argument that the Roman Catholic tradition was potentially deeply congruent with American democracy, are well
known.[7] But from the perspective of American patterns of
behavior, Volume II may be much more revealing.[8]
Throughout a series of chapters, religion in America is
repeatedly identified as a part of the fabric of social and
political life, or the emerging American culture. More
explicit reflections on this issue were offered by Michael
Chevalier, whose visit in the middle of the 1830s to inspect
public works in the United States also led to an analysis of
the society developing in the new world.[9]

Writing a letter from Bedford Springs, Pennsylvania,
"one of the American watering places," in August 1835,
Chevalier was moved to reflect on the boredom he observed at summer resorts in the new world. He thought
that the chief explanation was to be found in the inferiority
of the upper classes in America to those in Europe—a basic
theme of his book. But in passing, he offered some interesting observations about the need for festivals and
ceremonies among the multitude. This was an appetite
satisfied in Europe, in his judgment, by the richness of the
Roman Catholic cultural tradition.

Already [he observed] democracy, especially in the
Western States, is beginning to have its festivals,
which thrill its fibres, and stir it with agreeable
emotions.[10]

For Chevalier, the chief exhibit of this development was
"the Methodist camp-meetings." These were "religious
festivals . . . to which the people press with eager delight,
in spite of the philosophical remonstrances of the more
refined sects. . . . Besides the camp-meetings, the political processions are the only things in this country, which

bear any resemblance to festivals."[11] He went on to explain that "the American, then, has become poor in ideality, in proportion as he has become rich in material wealth." (The estimate of high culture in America shared by Americans!)

Chevalier was confident that the cultural impoverishment would be overcome in the end: "But I am sure that America will have her festivals, her ceremonies, and her art, as I am that society in America will assume a regular organization."[12] The line of analysis developed in this study agrees with this judgment. It does, however, assume more of an instrumental relationship between the achievement of "festivals, ceremonies and art" and the "regular organization" of society than may be implied in Chevalier's observation.

Chevalier's comments assumed the distinction we have noted between high and popular culture. But while his prejudices favored the first, he no less recognized the importance of the latter if any people or nation were to have what we would term an identity. Moreover, he made it amply clear that the society-supporting culture of festivals and ceremonies (the absence of which he laments) must finally be recognized as closely associated with, or even derived from, religion. This is the sense in which a genuine American culture, patterns of behavior reflecting distinctive national characteristics, is so elusive to the historian. As the nation was coming to be, in its first incarnation after the Revolution and in its second after the Civil War, it lacked a cadre of field anthropologists to locate, describe, and analyze the behavioral aspect of the developing culture.

For this reason, our discussion will proceed by seeking to identify basic patterns of behavior in contemporary political and social life which appear to be continuous with past American practices. One line of approach will be to develop a crude inventory of the various kinds of behavior patterns which seem to impart a ritual structure to the national life in a way that might be evidence for piety toward the nation. A second line of approach will be to give attention to a logically separate question, whether the reality of particular ritual patterns entails as a necessary postulate the existence of a differentiated public religion. Our conclusion will resemble that reached on the basis of reviewing linguistic material in the last chapter: this behavioral material permits the argument to be advanced that there is substantial civic piety in the culture. But it requires careful interpretation in terms of theoretical constructs and does not necessarily mean that public religion exists as a positive tradition or cultural institution.

An inventory may be fundamentally flawed in two different ways: errors of categorization and basic incompleteness. Especially in attempting to review such a vast and largely uncharted wilderness as American social behavior, these flaws represent hazards so serious as to call into question the proposed exercise. For this reason, our procedure will be to attempt to identify several sets of discrete patterns. First we will note those that seem to express most directly, and representatively, patterns of behavior symbolically linked to the reality of the nation— in short, those which might most convincingly be interpreted as elements of civic religious practice. It will then be appropriate to move from the more confidently interpreted phenomena to those that are less securely construed in this way. Thus, the claims made with respect to the latter, at least in some impressionistic sense, can be checked or tried out against data more securely identified in our framework of analysis.

At the center of the civic ritual structure lie those patterns of behavior identified with the continuity of political offices. These include rituals which provide for the routine assumption of continuing offices by new occupants. This is a structure insuring orderly transition from one incumbent to another, as well as making provision for extraordinary transfer of authority. Construed narrowly, the swearing in of a new president is a ritually limited act. On first reflection, it is a symbolically barren event which can be traced to the origin of our political system in a context broadly suffused with both Calvinistic and Enlightenment rationalism. Behind the central event (a simple oath of office sworn on a Bible before the representatives of the other major branches of government) stands the pattern of oath-taking based on Biblical prohibitions. This contrasts, for example, with the protracted, traditional, and symbol-laden pageantry through which the succession of traditional monarchies is assured. In the first years of the new republic, comparatively little elaboration seems to have taken place. The ritual transfer of authority stood isolated from any penumbra of celebration and secondary ritual elaboration. (We are informed, as an example, that Jefferson walked to his inauguration in New York City from a boarding house. Following the brief ceremony, he returned to eat his supper at his lodgings.[13] Indeed, it is reported that by virtue of his unusual lateness, he was forced to wait his turn to eat.) For all the accretion of other elements through the nation's history, the ritual center of the transfer of office has remained securely located in this stark and rational ceremony—which is cast in sharp relief by the events surrounding unanticipated transfers of power. With the assassination of President John F. Kennedy, Vice President Lyndon B. Johnson was elevated to the office under emergency conditions—in the cabin of an airplane poised on a runway. The oath of office was sworn before an otherwise unknown but available federal judge pressed into service in the absence of the Chief Justice of the Supreme Court.[14] The central ritual elements stood starkly isolated and were few indeed: participation by the individual assuming office, a representative of the legal system symbolizing social and political continuity, the oath taken with hand raised, and a copy of the sacred scriptures to assure truthfulness. That no challenge to President Johnson's legitimacy was remotely conceived indicates the secure place of this ritual pattern within the culture.

Much the same set of elements is central to the ritual through which lesser civic officers (both elected and appointed) are installed, and it pertains to virtually all branches of government at state, county, and local levels. The oath is sworn by the presumptive incumbent before a representative of already existing, and usually continuing, legitimacy. The intention of the individual is proved by the presence of the sacred object (most usually a book). This signifies a binding commitment to discharge the obligations of the office and to maintain the integrity of the regime. The particular elements—for example, the wording of the oath of office and the specified representation of legitimacy—vary depending upon the office in question. It would only be in an active fantasy-life that the member of the local school board would confuse his or her installation with that of a city mayor, a state governor, or the president. But the formal ritual elements and the relationships between them represent a common structure deeply imbedded in the culture.

So thoroughly is the culture imbued with this pattern, it carries over into the ceremonies of installation for extra-governmental positions. Various educational, religious, and charitable institutions provide for the installations of their officers with variations of the same ceremonial elements. These may be elaborated at great length and enriched with additional elements, or they may be condensed to the basic set required. Indeed, benign and malignant voluntary societies (for instance, the Red Cross and the Ku Klux Klan) share the same *basic* ceremonial pattern to assure successful transfer of authority from one generation of leaders to the next. (It may be that the pattern was first fully developed in the context of voluntary groups and only subsequently extended to republican governments. But this point anticipates later stages of the chapter.) What concerns us is not the genesis of the ritual pattern—that is easy enough to set out, at least in basic terms. Nor is it important to emphasize the slight variations in fundamentals—the Bible may not be universally used, the candidate may have been selected through various means, and the legitimacy may be interpreted in numerous ways. In our framework, chief interest is in the virtual universality of a ceremonial pattern appearing in numerous and widely divergent contexts throughout the society. It is quite clearly this fundamental structure which gives social significance to the particular ceremonies. This important point requires elaboration.

The immediate social context for rituals establishing transfer of the presidential office to the next incumbent involves a festive and celebrative setting. It is a demonstration of either confirmation in office of a political party, or the effective replacement of a chief competitor. Thus, friends, associates, well-wishers, and aspirants for favors all use the occasion to display pronounced regional and party loyalties. This pattern seems to have evolved rapidly in the political life of the new nation once it became clear that political parties were necessary to the infant republic. Howevermuch the president might need to appear above partisanship once in office, he could gain office only on the basis of party effort. So the ceremony surrounding the inauguration imparts to it a precise meaning in the context of political struggle. Further the ceremony indicates that it is to be seen as a concluding act in the drama of the American electoral process. The ritual installation completes a story which starts years beforehand as a candidate begins to seek the presidency. President Carter's is a textbook case of the struggle for support, party nomination, and final victory.

The basic elements of the inauguration are manifestly ritualized expressions of American life. But they are ritual behavior no more so than the stylized patterns of behavior in the preceding process. While substantial effort is devoted to developing party support for a candidate and securing his nomination, an image of a candidate is created to indicate his appeal to various constituencies based upon class, status, ethnic, or regional loyalties. (Great care is taken to gauge the responses of these electoral groups.) The image is created on the basis of a pattern of appearances among representatives of such groups. This pattern is so ingrained in the behavior of American political aspirants as to be taken for granted. It is no less true for candidates in local elections than it is among those who aspire to the White House. While changes have occurred at a superficial level—for instance, utilization of different means of travel (an airplane instead of a train or horse-drawn carriage) and cultivation of new media (television instead of newspapers)—there has not been significant change in the deep pattern involved. The cultural basis of the pattern is thrown into sharp relief when an American incumbent, or an aspirant, goes abroad and instinctively knows no other pattern of behavior. The transfer to an alien setting of American rituals—seeking to "meet the people" in Soviet Russia or China, for instance, in ways

quite foreign to the political rituals of those nations—
makes the point perfectly. The attempt to use American
electoral methods is no less culturally innovative when, for
instance, a politician attempts to introduce patterns common in the United States into French politics.[15]

It might be objected that this penumbra of activities,
setting a wider context for the central rituals concerned
with transfer of power, ought not to be identified as fully
ritualized behavior. At the very least, however, we must
recognize codes of behavior which are culturally constraining and which function, at least as basically as strictly
linguistic phenomena, to establish and maintain American society.[16] What appears to be involved is a pattern of
presentation and acceptance/rejection, or of promise and
support/declination. This nexus is so elementary, and so
much does it resemble a broader range of social transactions (for example, the merchandising exchanges in the
society at large), that we readily slip into language about it
derived from the marketplace. Candidates "sell" themselves, electorates "buy" a program or have it "sold" to
them, "killings" are made (in the language of the stock
market, not of war)—the list could be extended indefi-
nitely from the experiences readily available to all of us. In
this observation, we approach directly a crucial insight for
purposes of this study. While it is procedurally necessary
to isolate within a social matrix various species of behavior,
they are not as differentiated in the culture as economic,
political, religious, and other frameworks of analysis pre-
suppose. That there are culturally common codes of behavior which run through our society is basic to the
present analysis. Later, we will return to this point, but
first another pattern requires attention.

A second fundamental elaboration of political behavior
in terms of ritual codes requires brief notice. This is the

ceremonial (or ritual) constraint upon the relationship of office-holder to citizens. As in the case of ritual patterns underlying the struggle for and assumption of office, the cultural pattern is manifested in a range of levels of social organization, from presidential State visits to local inspection tours by a mayor's deputy. What deserves attention about this range of phenomena is the different pattern present in it. The pattern of presentation and acceptance/rejection characterizes the relationship between candidates (and their supporters), on the one hand, and the electorate on the other. This second pattern, then, involves the officeholder representing authority to which the appropriate response is deference on the part of the constituent. In basic respects, this is a much more authoritarian pattern, reflecting the reality of power and the recognition of status. This pattern is very ancient and continues the code underlying, for example, ceremonies surrounding behavior in a monarchical society. It is authoritarian insofar as it is rooted in submission. In the American version or development of the pattern, however, the rejection of authority is generally tolerated culturally so long as civil order is not directly threatened. The demonstration and the sit-in, especially as elaborated in the late 1960s, orchestrated the expressions of denial to the point of a seeming rejection of authority altogether. The political power of the demonstration or the sit-in was thus directly derived from the challenge mounted to a prevailing cultural pattern.[17]

Up to this point, the present chapter has proposed that we may identify characteristic behavior patterns central to the continuation of American social life in its political aspect. One pattern can be observed in the relationship between candidates and possible constituencies. A second pattern governs the specific transfer of power and authority. A third pattern concerns relationships between officeholders and the general public. These patterns of behavior are basic to American society. While not unique to it, they have undergone distinctive development in America so as to constitute a culture of political behavior which must be viewed as central to the question of civic piety.

A second location for ritual and ceremonial elements in American culture is possibly more obvious, while at the same time being less sharply delineated than the patterns concerned with public offices. These are the celebrative and commemorative events of the national life. Within the civil religion discussion to date, considerable attention has been given to ceremonial aspects of American life as evidence for a national religion. Conrad Cherry, for example, drew attention to Memorial Day as a celebration of civil religion, basing his discussion on practices in Boalsburg, Pennsylvania, which claims to be the place of origin of this cultural event.[18] He also effectively reviewed the phenomenon of the virtually spontaneous and widespread grief-stricken response to the assassination of Senator Robert Kennedy—and, by implication, the deaths of President John F. Kennedy and the Reverend Martin Luther King—as manifestations of a religious aspect of the national identity.[19] These events are within the recent memory of many of us. Full accounts and widespread analysis of them have made them accessible to virtually all. It is not difficult to identify other parallel observances which, while not a part of the experience of so many, nonetheless seem to belong to this same genus and thus might properly be interpreted within the same framework. The celebrations of victory at the conclusion of World War II were occasions of national rejoicing in the 1940s, even as the senseless violent deaths of national leaders were occasions for spontaneous national mourning in the 1960s.[20] For earlier generations, the armistice to end World War I was occasion for ecstasy. In that case, what began as a one-time celebration was transformed into an annual event celebrated until recent years on November 11. Armistice Day has lately and dramatically lost social significance.[21]

It is possible, of course, to write a natural history of these and other cultural celebrations of major events from the very beginnings of national life to the present. Each one of them occasioned the clarification of national identity. Apparently, certain events are experienced, or perceived retrospectively, as having symbolic importance in the development of collective life. Some illustrations are the birth of the founder, the violent death of a beloved leader, the termination of a bloody struggle, and the augmentation of the national territory. Initially, the emotional response to a particular event leads almost spontaneously to collective acknowledgement within the society. Finally, action is taken on behalf of the whole. Doubtless this sequence of responses reinforces the collectivity and, for example, enables it to survive the inevitable transitional period when a society organized for war undertakes to face a future without such a determinate and proximate goal. Once experienced, some commemorative events flourish and retain their hold or power for a considerable span of years. Others wither in short order, apparently failing to stir the collective imagination or focus the emotional stirrings of the society for a significant span of time. The length, the intensity, and the geographical extension of the celebration depend upon whether its social occasion remains a symbolic threat to social solidarity, whether it has come to serve other interests, or whether it has become appropriated to the purposes of particular interest groups.[22] It is difficult to deny the importance of such manifestations of collective consciousness and self-consciousness in American self-definition. Certainly, there are many exceedingly close parallels to other societies, for all societies face comparable issues.

What requires analysis at this point is not the natural history of such events as a type or the reality of particular social ritual events, whether occasional or repeated. The question arising in this study is how such material ought to be interpreted in relationship to the question of American public religion. Specifically, what religious significance does this class of phenomena possess? Does it, at one extreme, represent evidence for a diffused civic piety, or, at the other, for a particular civil religion focused on the current national polity?

It can be argued in a manner parallel to one side of Robert Bellah's interpretation of presidential inaugural addresses that we might discover a ritual horizon (pattern or framework) for the national life in this kind of behavior. From such a point of view, civic piety exists as a reality at the threshold of consciousness, if not below it, and is only vaguely perceived from time to time by members of the society as self-conscious behavior. Thus its relatively *ad hoc* and episodic character is not an argument for its weakness, but is precisely a mark of its hold on the society.[23] On the basis of this approach, the fact that it is largely implicit rather than explicit indicates its decisive importance for the society. While such a position should not be dismissed out of hand, precisely because it is plausible, we should not be deflected from the attempt at more sustained and serious understanding of this ceremonial and ritual behavior in a broader framework.

What seems to occur in such ceremonies is the dramatic demonstration that the social or collective life of a particular group is subject to a wide range of specific boundaries in space and time. What might these be? The most extensive relevant analysis of American social ceremonies continues to be that developed by W. Lloyd Warner and his associates as a part of their Yankee City series.[24] The concluding, fifth volume studies the symbolic life of Newburyport, Massachusetts. Although published in the 1950s, the book was largely based on an earlier decade (the 1930s). The social context is marked by regional peculiarities; Newburyport is a multi-ethnic, seacoast town north of Boston. On the basis of the evidence available, however, the general issues and the theoretical insights achieved should be applicable much more broadly to American society. Careful analysis of comparable events in other American communities would probably permit useful analysis of similar patterns. What becomes clear in Warner's study is that while explicit national or American symbols are present in the celebration of Memorial Day in Newburyport and might at one level be properly interpreted as constituting its meaning, at other no less significant levels different kinds of symbolic elements and rituals are oriented both to more universal and to more particular issues in concurrent individual and collective lives within the community. In sum, the content of Memorial Day in Yankee City, and, by extension, comparable events in other communities as well, is not exhausted by analysis of civic piety (let alone a civil religion), however much that model could provide for an explicit interpretation of the event.

At the most general level, Warner interprets Memorial Day in Yankee City as a symbolic confrontation with death—the death which stands as a final limitation to the life of every individual human. In more regional and local frameworks, the celebrations expressly recognize the patterns of superior and inferior status in the relationships between ethnic groups constituting the social life of the town. Thus, while indicating the importance of the ritual celebration to the community life of Yankee City, Warner's analysis of Memorial Day suggests that a complex analysis must be undertaken. More reflective students of American life recognize that the celebrative and commemorative occasions are inherently rich when developed into social rituals. In addition, the rituals embody far more complex references than would seem to be required if they were simply interpreted as evidence for a civic cult or a religion centered on the national polity.

Were superior ethnographic materials readily available, much the same point would probably emerge with reference to most ceremonial events which have marked the life of the national community. While, for example, Fourth of July celebrations routinely make manifest rhetorical reference to national independence, other elements seem to be extremely important in the actual ritual development of the day. The full extent of the day as a social occasion is suggested by the prominent role of voluntary societies (a central observation made by Warner in his discussion of Memorial Day); for example, they sponsor fireworks and organize sports events which have no explicit reference to the national community. When viewed as representing the extensive festivals that Chevalier anticipated these ceremonial events indicate the basic parameters of social life in America. In this perspective, Washington's Birthday, another example, appears in a different light. On the one hand, the holiday manifestly celebrates the legendary virtues of the "father of his country." But in its modern development, through ubiquitous merchandising spectaculars, it establishes the ideal of consumption as the basic means of participation in American society. The purchase of goods is announced as the sacramental act defining citizenship. To make the fundamental point in a theoretical manner, this genre of event has a basic ritual significance to the culture. This significance is definition of community in terms of limits, internal structures, and the conditions through which membership in it is available. We are suggesting that it is necessary to see these broader patterns of behavior and the virtues attendant upon them as condensed in the central ceremonial or ritual patterns of American life. These patterns count far more than abstract liberal values (independence, freedom, civic loyalty, etc.) in the definition of the community.

In seeking to identify basic patterns of religio-political behavior in American society, we first looked to the central political phenomena of the culture and reviewed the provision for fundamental continuities in offices through a ritual pattern of behavior centering on two movements. One of these may be described in general terms as the aspirants' presentations of self to the people, who in turn indicate acceptance or rejection. A second movement is the presentation of self by incumbents. The conventional response is deference, although strategies of denial have been common in the recent past. We then turned to analyze the celebrative and commemorative structuring of time, which makes manifest reference to events of the nation but may embody far more powerful latent patterns, namely that of community definition and the possibility of its periodic rejuvenation. Finally, a more generalized set of patterns of behavior must be noted. These concern the routine ordering of social life organized in the broadest sense and have reference to the government of the common life. Viewed in a strictly behavioral framework, the individual and collective lives of Americans embody high and low rituals. Through participation in the latter, Americans demonstrate their individual and collective identification in terms of the common social system, and they assent to the life it enables them to live. It is a kind of fealty extracted from the public, a continuing reaffirmation of incorporation into and dependence upon the general community of American life, as well as one or more constitutive sub-communities.

In such a perspective, elections and other referenda are the most obvious and clear-cut instances of low rituals, repeated symbolic acceptance of the system. Viewed rationally, voting by each individual influences the outcome of a contest for office in only the most marginal fashion or under conditions of an extremely close issue. But viewed in the perspective of social exchanges, the willingness to make a choice, or at least to register to do so, is a strong behavioral commitment to the social system of the community. In terms of the society's coherence, that is to say, the primordial loyalties which Verba posited, the latent aspect of behavior is far more significant than its manifest content. From this point of view, the systems of criminal and administrative laws with their attendant bureaucracies which require patterns of behavior and exact numerous minor penalties serve similar functions. Of course, this behavioral level is beneath the more immediately rational understandings which explain the system to its members. In these terms the symbolic aspects of mundane transactions are focused: the traffic ticket (requiring at least a payment to the municipality, an appearance in its court, or, alternatively, acting out the role of scofflaw), the litigation over the terms of divorce, the toll payment to a quasi-governmental agency for use of a bridge or roadway, the inspection of the passport at the national border, and sales and income taxes. All these and countless other routines of everyday life are certainly rational transactions in a highly differentiated and structured social order. But they are also symbolic acts defining the real claims made upon all of us by the many and overlapping communities which sustain the rich and variegated collective life of American society. They are instances of continual and direct ritual acknowledgement of the authority on which the society is based.

Viewed in this perspective, those patterns of behavior through which individuals explicitly interact with government agencies merge imperceptibly into patterns of behavior which concern the private sector of life as well. Merchandising spectaculars, especially in the setting of a sluggish economy, take on aspects of required patriotic participation.[25] The entertainment industry also elicits distinctive patterns of behavior which confirm membership in the culture. On reflection, these behaviors, which are more strictly economic or social, seem to be continuous with behavior in the public realm. All of them have at least latent significance as social ritual—a theme repeatedly suggested in the foregoing pages.

The present conventional life of American society is being reoriented away from towns and cities toward peripheral or regional shopping and cultural centers, a development with important behavioral implications for the ritual basis of American society. Even apparently dissenting acts from the dominant culture—alternate vacations such as camping at the Cape Cod National Seashore, in Yellowstone National Park, or wilderness backpacking in Northern Maine—prove on inspection to be sub-cultures thoroughly linked to the broader society. National parks supervised by public employees provide the setting. The sporting goods industry not only prescribes necessary equipment but establishes a culture of proper equipment. A network of volunteers stands ready to mobilize support in emergencies. What may look and feel like individual independence asserted against the culture turns out to be dramatization of a deeper cultural identity.

Some of these issues will reemerge and be explored in greater detail in subsequent chapters. The present point is that we should not imagine that patterned behavior in the public realm with its ritual implications is discontinuous with patterned behavior in the private sector or in personal life. In terms of ritualized interaction, citizens are bound to the society in countless ways quite below the threshold of normal self-consciousness. These are the levels of behavioral loyalty to which Verba called attention. The primordial bonds which he identified must be located in such a manner. If there is a religious aspect of American polity, analysis of it must be carried on by giving sustained attention to these phenomena.

The argument of this chapter has been relentlessly straightforward to this point. In effect, it has been that there are patterns of behavior in American culture with respect to government of the society which have ceremonial or ritual aspects. These concern, in a word, the maintenance of society. This issue is all the more difficult to prove because our highly rationalistic explanation or theory of political life is biased more toward manifest than toward latent interpretations of individual and collective behavior. The issue is not *whether* there exist ritual aspects of American social life which might be identified as elements of civic piety. Exist they do and in great profusion. (At the same time in form or pattern there seem to be only a few basic types of interaction.)

The central issue is the arbitrariness of identifying only a certain *restricted* class of ceremonial events as the ritual material of American social life—inauguration ceremonies, Memorial Day celebrations, spontaneous days of mourning for public figures, and so forth. This issue is complicated by the claim that this class is evidence for a positive and differentiated civil religion. Such reasoning is transparently circular, although it is consistent with discussion of religious ritual in much theoretical literature. The particular argument would be more compelling if a discrete class of ritual activities celebrating the reality of American society stood apart and did not clearly merge into patterns of behavior obviously not part of a differentiated national cult.

In sum, if the manifest ritual events of American political life are the basis for arguing that a differentiated civil religion exists, then the much more inclusive set of patterned behaviors continuous with those ceremonies poses a problem. But if the significance is thought to be in that broad range of patterned behavior, then that argues for a very different interpretation. The diffusion of ceremony is not a compelling argument for the existence of a differentiated civil religion. We conclude that the symbolic life of American communities seems to be less manifestly differentiated into a class of religious rituals than is required by the hypothesis that a well-institutionalized civil religion actually exists. Insofar as it is possible to judge, this seems to have been true throughout American history.

From one perspective, this conclusion represents a kind of dead end: it calls into question the identification of a special realm of behavior with a civic cult in the same way that close analysis of presidential addresses and declarations discovers them to be equivocal with respect to the question of whether the president becomes, in one guise at least, an oracle of national belief and guardian of its mysteries. But this argument from ceremonial behavior does open up quite another line of inquiry. If society is so thoroughly characterized by patterns of behavior which constitute its real culture, must we not recognize in the particular patterns a distinctive set which should be viewed as such? These might be recognized as a powerful ingredient in the basic national identity. In such a perspective, the particular differentiating characteristics in American society have little to do with the manifest content of special events or with references made by special symbols. The central subject is the style or pattern which characterizes virtually the whole range of behavior within the society. This kind of viewpoint calls further into question any concept of a differentiated national religion. It does suggest, however, that there are lines of exploration which might be followed in pursuing Verba's observation that a primordial (religious) commitment to society underlies explicit political interaction.

An inquiry along these lines would need to draw heavily upon work in anthropology which has studied ritual in terms of process.[26] In particular, it might use a proposal made by Mary Douglas in her study, *Natural Symbols.*[27] She argued for the analysis of any culture in terms of the relationship between "group" and "grid"—that is, between the strength of group bonds and the prominence of defined roles and rules within any given society. The relationship between those patterns, she suggested, is most directly expressed in a body symbolism unique to each society. Theoretically, it ought to be possible to interpret any society within such a framework. She argues that explanatory models of society (for instance, sociological ones) which posit social change, stress, "compensation," or other "causes" as the framework of analysis are inadequate. They neither offer explanations valid under different circumstances nor permit identification of more basic and persisting patterns quite independent of circumstances usually thought to be casual. The group/grid analysis, she argues, does make possible useful comparison between cultures and across social systems (pre-literate to advanced industrial societies) conventionally believed to be incomparable. In the present essay, the intention is not to criticize, refine, defend, or report in detail her stimulating proposal. Rather, the point is to pick up the suggestion that we might find at deep levels of social interaction one or more coherent patterns of behavior defining the American culture. This is an alternative analytical program to that which has absorbed so much attention in the civil religion discussion—namely, rehearsing the limited and somewhat ambiguous evidence for explicit civil religious ritual and ceremonial behavior in the American context. On balance, this framework offers a far more promising approach than the attempt to identify convincingly a differentiated civil religion in the undergrowth of American symbols.

One outcome of this perspective confirms a point of view which has been implicit throughout this chapter and which must be fully spelled out at its end. On this view, any analysis of American social life in terms of a symbol system must survey, even as Lloyd Warner did, materials well beyond the political or even public range of ritual behavior conventionally associated with patriotism to the national community. In this framework, ritual patterns are suffused through personal no less than social life. This holds for the American and every other setting. In our contemporary society, the business, merchandising, entertainment, sports, political, and religious worlds must be viewed as interpenetrating each other with related ritual forms and an essentially common content. The similarity in the codes underlying these apparently differentiated worlds helps to explain why success in one proves readily transferable to others—the athletic star becoming a successful businessman or entertainer, the proven businessman finding a ready welcome in politics, and so on. The codes underlying the separate careers are similar, and the contents are finally identical. Thus, specific roles in American society seem always to have been relatively interchangeable since our first soldier/president. The American set, or combination of grid and group, embodies particular age-defining roles and pressures typical of a relatively secular cosmology. The American society is extensive enough and sufficiently complex internally to exclude the possibility that it might as a whole embody, except perhaps episodically, a more exclusively group or grid pattern.

In any case, the outcome of the present chapter is further confirmation of a skeptical attitude toward any claim that a particular social ritual in American culture can be identified simply as an instance of civic piety. This is not only because the ritual or ceremonial occasions which might be viewed as the most likely exhibits are not univocal in their references to the nation and its polity. Memorial Day, Fourth of July, and like holidays make references more general and more local than a civil religion would require. It is also because it appears theoretically arbitrary to separate any particular ritual from the matrix of patterned behavior which *is* American culture. If our most basic insight is that a primordial attachment lies at the basis of the social order, then by implication it is no more valid to separate rituals exclusively constitutive of public religion than it is to identify a national ideology composed of the linguistic materials surveyed in the last chapter.

Chapter 5

RELIGIOUS MEANINGS
OF THE AMERICAN COMMUNITY

Communities are formed and sustained through common language usage and patterns of behavior which give definition to social orders. They may also be viewed in terms of shared meanings which provide frameworks of self-understanding for individual and collective life. These social meanings may concern aspects of human life such as suffering, evil, or death traditionally explained in religious terms. Or they may be held as basic or primordial orientations to the world (other-worldly contemplation, this-worldly activism, and so forth). At the very least such frameworks of intelligibility function as if they were religious, and their significance for individuals and groups makes it difficult to distinguish them from religion. Recent anthropological literature helps to make it clear that whatever other characteristics it has religion provides a horizon for social life because it addresses questions of origins and destinies, individual and collective motivations and purposes, and issues of consequences over time. On the one hand, this insight suggests that traditional religions have served important functions in American society. On the other, identifying this kind of function also suggests that other meanings than those necessarily associated with positive religious traditions may have had important cognate roles to play in American social life.

For these reasons, it is important to review the major

meanings attributed to America. Some have drawn on traditional religions—for example, identification of the American nation as a new order in the world, or the American experience as the culmination of world history. But others have more immediately secular sources, such as America's receptivity to the poor and rejected of the world. But whether originating in recognized religious traditions or Enlightenment idealism, these meanings (or appropriated symbols) have become quasi-religious aspects of the culture. They image the world socially constructed in America. Finally, they establish the frameworks of social life, directly influence individual behavior, and shape social interaction. In this general perspective, it is not likely that we will discover evidence for a monovalent and highly coherent national meaning system. Rather, we might expect to discover a series of meanings or large-scale frameworks of intelligibility which have been influential in American social life from time to time because espoused by divergent groups for different apparent purposes in significantly varying constructions. We may expect to discover a cluster of interpretations of American society which have appeared at different points in our national history and have entered into different combinations within it. In short, we may view American culture as characterized by religious meanings.

In an analysis of this symbolic framework of national life, it is not important to delineate the entire set, so to speak, but rather to identify major elements in the series and to indicate how they have appeared in different guises—that is, under different social circumstances. The set of symbols so identified gives a particular identity to the American society, although the elements constituting this set need not be unique to the national experience. Of course, such a set of meanings would necessarily be coherent; that is, it would not embody unresolvable contradictions between the separate elements. But such a religious dimension of American life must be understood as internally differentiated; that is, as the expression of a religiously pluriform culture.

The particular constellation of religious meanings we will review below includes the following major elements:

1. American society understood as perfected and pure, unalloyed and uncompromised. In contrast to the societies of the old world and antiquity, it requires of its members internalized discipline.

2. American society as fulfillment of the dreams and aspirations of the ages, frequently exhibited in historical categories and under eschatalogical symbols, and held forth in millenarian language.

3. American society as receptive to the deprived and the homeless of the world, and promising them new life.

4. American society as one of opportunity in which liberty provides the framework for individual and collective development.

These four clusters of meaning certainly do not exhaust the list that could be compiled. It is probably the case, however, that additional meanings which might be identified would prove to be consonant with or subsumed under one or more of these. Furthermore, there is potential for tension among them—for example, the quest for perfection and purity has at times made American society relatively unreceptive to outsiders. Alternatively they may function in mutually inclusive ways—the achievement of liberty is often imaged as the precise content of the millennium. But these sets of symbols are each central enough and yet discrete enough to warrant close attention. At the same time, they have been associated in different groupings. The same central meaning has taken on different shading or coloration in separate periods of history and subgroups of American society. In this way, rather different operative clusters of meaning have been constituted. Accordingly, the approach adopted here has the special virture of accepting the great variety of empirical social meanings which have or had significance in America. These are cultural givens which cannot be overlooked. For this reason, our approach is also a means of attempting to deal with the difficult interpretive problem of unities and diversities in American society, at least as expressed in religious terms. Therefore this kind of approach should prove to be a means of moving beyond the rather fruitless discussions of interpretive frameworks in American religious history which argue, for example, that there is either a dominant Puritan axis to the American experience or a central Enlightenment core.[1]

One pronounced framework of intelligibility in American culture has been derived from the concern, some would say obsession, with purity, or a perfected society. It is important to reflect on this issue with some care because we characteristically assume a conventional perspective in which the history of American society is one of progressive liberation from the legacy of Puritanism—the latter defined as obsessive concern with more perfect control over selves and the social order. Cast in this way, the basic struggle in American culture is thought to have been between Puritans and liberals. The valences of good and evil have been assigned to both parties, depending upon the particular preferences of the one undertaking the interpretation. Quite clearly, however, such an approach presupposes a bipolar framework, and it is more productive to adopt an open-ended, pluralistic approach to the phenomena. The place to begin may not be with the Puritans *per se* but with the critical observation that there have been a variety of specific puritanisms in American history.

This is a topic that intrigued Marcus Lee Hansen, finally prompting him to write an essay in which he explicitly reflected on the question.[2] Should we, he asked, attribute so much influence to the New England Puritans of the seventeenth century? Should they be held responsible for the commitment to greater purity which surfaces from time to time thoroughout American history—among Roman Catholic clerical leaders, for example, who embrace the cause of temperance, or among Lutherans who have little use for the rationalism of the Reformed ecclesiastical tradition, or among sects like the Unification Church in contemporary American society? On reflection, it turns out that the descendants of the original Puritans have as frequently as not been associated with liberal causes and have been hostile to later puritanisms. On the other hand, the representatives of very different religious traditions in which there may have been little if any puritanism previously expressed have frequently sought a purer and stricter way—that is, have turned out to be puritans.

What Marcus Hansen went on to propose was a link between puritanism as the concern for stricter patterns of behavior in whatever realm and the related commitment to fundamental moral goals, and the condition of migration into the American society.[3] It is frequently overlooked that migration has been the *defining characteristic of American society* from the seventeenth century to the middle of the twentieth, and the ramifications of the process continue to the present and will probably continue into the future. As the first serious student of immigration in American social history, Hansen had chiefly in mind the phenomenon of transplantation from another society to the new continent and the processes of acculturation and assimilation which inevitably are aspects of the adjustment to a new society. It is generally thought that the massive cumulative influx of migrants to America from virtually all the continents of the globe in the course of some three centuries is an wholly unparalleled event in human history, although it may be possible to identify intense migrations over a short span of time comparable in scale.[4] In the American case, the overall migration was composed of numerous particular migrations displaying great variety in the characteristics of the immigrant groups. At one extreme has been the large number of Africans seized from their own societies in brutal ways and transported to a life of slavery in the new world.[5] At the other might be that small group of French who fled from the revolution in their own nation and entered into the society of the new United States at a relatively secure stratum, able to preserve many of the privileges that would have been summarily removed at home. The scale, intensity, and duration of migration have also varied greatly from one group to another. Compare the massive and relatively intensive migration from Eastern Europe with the continuing slow trickle of migrants from England. (For the latter, the Atlantic crossing and adjustment to the new society in both the colonial and national periods was relatively undemanding.) The various facets of the overall process are staggering and have contributed in numerous direct and indirect ways to the making of America.

As important as this migration to the United States has been the related phenomenon of continuing internal migration which remains essentially unchecked. Most obvious and taken for granted has been the large scale redistribution of black Americans. Until the end of the nineteenth century, the black community was a predominantly southern and rural sub-culture. By the middle of the twentieth century, however, black Americans had migrated to form the core of virtually all the cities of the north.[6] There is now some evidence to suggest that this movement has begun to reverse, and that a return of American blacks to a revitalized south is beginning on a significant scale. But other internal shifts of population have gone on concurrently, and if they are less immediately visible they are not less striking. At the present time, demographic studies indicate not only a continuation of the general pattern of frequent movement, but a decisive shift of the population and social power (economic) away from older, largely northern urban complexes toward an arc of states stretching from the Atlantic Ocean to the Pacific and encompassing a sunbelt, or a "southern rim."[7] The kinds of specific political strategies which may have been launched on the basis of this perception do not concern us. What does is the essential continuity in the conditions of social life between the pattern of internal migrations in the middle of the twentieth century and earlier patterns of migration, including transitions to the new nation and movement within it (for example, the opening of successive frontiers until new land was exhausted at the end of the nineteenth century). Still other kinds of social movement go on, of course, including advancement and decline in social status. None of these migrations, if that may serve as the generic label, *necessarily* involves collective or group life, although that component is highly visible and obvious, as in the case of the blacks or in the attention given to the rapid self-conscious and publicized advancement in the social order of American Jews by the mid-twentieth century.[8]

Marcus Hansen proposed that there was a link between the continuing reality of immigration into American society and the puritanism which seemed to be so much a continuing aspect of American social history. His point was that almost without exception migration involved a group. The resulting stress for group life in coming to terms with a new environment produced leaders who generally sought to organize the collective life in more disciplined or rigorous terms so that a group would be more effective in the new social setting. It was also a strategy to appear to be less alien and thus less isolated from the continuing centers of power and influence in the new social setting. Under Hansen's analysis, therefore, puritanism was produced by the conditions of American social life. In this interpretation, puritanism is virtually inevitable as a social psychological response to the particular characteristics of American society. It turns out to have had instrumental or adaptive value in adjustment to the American social order. In sum, on this hypothesis puritanism is as proverbially American as apple pie.

Such a hypothesis is not easily tested in a definitive way, and it probably needs to be broadened and sharpened, since the American case is so internally diverse and extensive in space and time. But if, for purposes of this discussion, it is granted that internal migration in a social system of the scale and complexity of the American system is but a special case of migration more generally considered, and that migration is but a special case of social dislocation which might entail relative geographical stability but rapid social changes, we may then have achieved a formulation with a direct and immediate bearing upon our inquiry—the religious meanings of America. One implication of the hypothesis would be that puritanisms would be unlikely to develop within relatively stable social orders, while leaders committed to social purity and puritan movements in general would frequently emerge and prove to be influential under conditions of rapid social changes. To reach for contemporary examples, such a framework helps to explain why Scandanavian societies are, by general consent, almost devoid of puritan movements, indeed of puritan impulses. At the same time, however, China, Kenya, and Cuba demonstrate pronounced puritan traits and have experienced the full rigors visited upon societies by puritan movements.[9] Application of the hypothesis to the American case suggests, for example, why in the Second Great Awakening there seems to have been little puritan revivalism among the tidewater whites in Virginia, by contrast to its prominence among the settlers of inner Appalachia. This perspective helps to explain the stridency of nativism in the turbulent north—let us say, in upper New York state.[10]

This digression should help to place in perspective the proposal that puritanism provides one basic set of symbols or meanings for America. This insight derives from Marcus Lee Hansen, although he should not be held responsible for its extension in the manner I have suggested. As one major strand of meaning in American social life, the image of a purified society has deep influence. Of course, as a set of symbols it is complex. The general meaning has included a concern, often exaggerated, to achieve control over those aspects of life experienced as uncertain. This uncertainty threatens individuals directly. Further, it challenges them indirectly through erosion of group identities based upon perceived collective interests. The quest for purity has been carried on in both private and public realms; consumption of alcoholic beverages, attitudes toward religious customs and traditions (especially as they stand in tension with general practices), patterns of sexual relationships, expectations governing participation in community affairs and numerous other areas of social life are behaviors that take place at the interfaces between groups and the broader society. Issues of this sort are especially prone to puritan constructions. In this sense puritanism is a stereotypical or coded response particularly characteristic of American society.

Puritanisms have provided one kind of religious meaning for American society. In the first instance, it has been a set of expectations about their own behavior that individuals and groups have adopted for themselves. In this sense it has concerned control of self and through discipline has become finally self-control. But frequently it has also included the aspect of control over other selves— that is, the exercise of social control over deviant individuals and groups. In this sense, puritanism presupposes a fundamentally authoritarian pattern of relationships within the world and reinforces that pattern. Thus, one of the basic sets of meaning through which American society explains itself to itself and to the world is in terms of the quest for purity, achievement of separation from the taint of the world and its concerns.

There are important ramifications to this orientation within the world. For instance, puritanisms are necessarily associated with essentially bipolar frameworks for conceiving of the world: good versus bad, us versus them. The puritan American while tightly disciplined is prone to be uncritical of self and hypercritical of others—both of those within the broader society who are different and of those external to the society altogether. Further, as puritanism originates in and continues to be fueled by the dynamics of social dislocation and change, its outcome will occasion additional change because it is an orientation in which individuals and groups do not rest easily with the world as they find it. Even relationships with other puritans may not be easy. Very simply, it is difficult for the puritan to live in the world.

As the commitment to a pure social order, puritanism has been one framework of national meaning, both subject to a variety of constructions and constitutive of the culture as a whole. No less has the idea of the millennium represented another strand in the rope of religious meaning in American society. Recent scholarship has manifested essentially two kinds of interest in millenarian developments in the setting of basically preliterate and traditional cultures. In such contexts, heightened anticipation of a period of perfection for the society has often been a response to natural disaster or asymmetrical and threatening relationships with a powerful or imperialistic society.[11] Historians, on the other hand, have had their interests kindled in particular millenarian movements, especially in Western societies. These movements have often been interpreted as the form taken by protest against the changing social order.[12] The symbols adopted for the social protest have usually been derived from the Judeo-Christian tradition in which the images of the anticipated end-state in history include the expectation of relief for the oppressed and achievement of justice for the persecuted. The term millennium refers to a belief that there will be a return of the Christ figure to preside over the hitherto persecuted elect for a penultimate period. Following the millennium the last judgement will take place and all things be consummated at the end of history. This powerful imagery serves to vest the outcome of history in the hands of the group suffering in one or another manner in the present.[13] In strict usage the term "millenarianism" refers to this complex of associated elements central to the tradition of Western religion. The term also denotes less fully elaborated interpretations of the historical process. For example, it is widely held that there will be general prosperity for the dispossessed and a rectification of previously suffered injustices in the coming of the millennium. When religious images function as social symbols in popular culture, they do not necessarily conform to the technical distinctions so important in more strictly theological usage.

What has been common to the millenarianism of preliterate cultures and to the social movements in Western history is the anticipation of better times in a determinate future—that is to say, in a period within the historical process, not beyond it, and believed to be near at hand. In the perspective of social psychology, millenarian beliefs have provided meaning for threatened cultures seeking to survive periods of great stress.[14]

A fundamental characteristic of modern America has been rapid, virtually perpetual, social change. Therefore, it is not surprising that, in the absence of a traditional class structure, millenarian movements should have developed from time to time in American social history.[15] Of course, particular episodes of millenarianism have been chronicled from the seventeenth century to the middle of the twentieth century. What is more interesting in the setting of the present discussion, however, is the place of generalized and durable millenarian social meanings. These latter appear to have served as significant frameworks of intelligibility within popular culture over relatively extended periods of time in American history. For example, scholarly attention has recently been drawn to the millenarian components which became influential with the Great Awakening (1740s) and continued through the late colonial and persisted into the early national periods. In studies of the phenomenon, it has been repeatedly suggested that such components played a critical role in the social preparation for the founding of the new nation in the latter decades of the eighteenth century. One author has pushed this thesis to the point of proposing that democratic Jacksonianism of the nineteenth century, virtually 100 years removed from the First Awakening in time, is properly interpreted as the secularized result of the millenarianism of the preceding period. Both movements envisioned polities more responsive to the claims of the people.[16]

The crusading impulse in American society, which has been prone repeatedly to identify one *final* evil to be eradicated or one *last* wrong to be righted, also embodies millenarian elements. The pattern originated in evangelical circles of the early nineteenth century in specific social reform movements. By the twentieth century, however, the form of the crusading appeal was deeply suffused through American political life. So the nation could have its entry into a world war plausibly explained as a "war to make the world safe for democracy." Equally plausible was the subsequent crusade against a great alternative world order, atheistic communism.[17]

The basic issue in this analysis is not whether any particular commitment be just or inherently good— whether the stand against a fundamental moral evil like slavery on the one hand is comparable in moral terms to that against a rather inevitable social convention like "demon rum" on the other. The point is that a particular pattern of religious meaning has penetrated American culture so as to shape decisively its basic style. So a resolution is repeatedly believed to be at hand to that one special evil which, when overcome, will permit a long-anticipated and presumably static era to be ushered in. It seems to be suggested that when the era is achieved, no more change will be necessary. Thus a deep sense of millenarian expectancy, admittedly with different specific contents, has suffused the American venture for more than three centuries. This pattern has a certain poignancy in a society so blessed with space, isolation (lack of immediate social threats), material resources beyond belief, and human talent. For all that America has nonetheless seemed to experience acutely a fear of failure. Thus in its uncertainty about internal coherence there has been frequent, even systematic, recourse to the myth of the better future, soon, in which the contradictions and threats of the present will be overcome.

One of the classic interpretations of American religious history is H. Richard Niebuhr's *The Kingdom of God in America.*[18] At one level, it is an exposition of the different interpretations placed upon the symbol of the Kingdom of God from colonial times to the early twentieth century. Niebuhr thought that generally there had been a pronounced movement from an emphasis upon the sovereignty of God over human affairs to an emphasis upon a Kingdom of Christ as normative for social relationships. This latter construction of the symbol was most explicitly undertaken in the Social Gospel movement in American Protestantism at the beginning of the twentieth century.[19] At another level, however, the study is the exploration of how the millenarian symbol of the Kingdom of God ties together much of American intellectual and social experience. More recently, a somewhat different approach to that theme has been offered in Ernest L. Tuveson's essay, *Redeemer Nation,* in which explicit attention is given to the national content of the millenarian symbol.[20] In whatever ways the symbol undergoes transformations in different periods and at different hands, its fundamental meaning is the attribution to the American nation of both external and internal redemptive roles in world history. In this sense millenarianism has been a root symbol of American life in the same way that puritanism has been. Of course, each of these basic religious meanings of American life has a number of facets and appears sometimes unexpectedly, in one avatar after another.

Although puritanism as a fundamental meaning of American culture may be traced to Protestant beginnings, it has become a generic characteristic of the society. In the same way, although millenarianism was predominantly associated with Protestantism at the outset, it has been transformed so as to pervade the whole—and most of the parts as well. Mormons of the 1850s and 1950s, Roman Catholic radicals of the 1880s and 1960s, followers of John Humphrey Noyes in the 1840s and of Sun Myung Moon in the 1970s all manifest the degree to which millenarianism as a style of cultural life is thoroughly distributed through the society and gives form to a complex set of meanings of American culture.

At the center of American millenarianism is an outrageous conviction that this society is but one step from a perfect order—or at least one step from a set of conditions under which stasis will be achieved. Thus, the millenarian component of social meaning is extremely dynamic, oriented to effect change, and insistent that change take place. Yet it simultaneously holds forth the assumption that the new era, the great society, the promised epoch will bring completion to the process. It is a compulsive framework, but also one which fosters internal divisions. The believer is oriented to act in ways thought to be contingent but necessary. Finally an outcome discontinuous with the present form of experience is promised. In sum, the framework of meaning is one in which the process of realizing a goal contradicts the content of that goal. It is a cultural version of the classical means-ends dilemma.

The religious meaning of American life is additionally complex because the millenarian symbol set exists not only in relationship to the puritanism already noted, but also in relationship to several other root meanings as well. The relationships between these meanings are not simple. To give an example, while in certain constructions the quest for purity can be imagined to be the content of the millennium, it is also possible for puritanism to value negatively the social commitments which symbolize the millenarian goal. Thus while there may be no place for race within the millennium, puritanisms may use race as an operative category of classification. Similar patterns of coincidence and conflict between the symbols exist with respect to additional basic meanings. These patterns make possible fundamental dissonance about the meaning of the society for members of different sub-cultures or different generations.[21] This potential for conflict and stress within the framework of social intelligibility will be more evident after we elaborate several other basic or root constructs of meaning within American culture.

Another location of religious meaning in American social life has been in the receptivity toward those who have fled other social orders and political regimes. America has been a new homeland for various kinds of groups, including refugees driven from homelands by war, oppression, famine, and social control. America's receptivity has been an internally complex symbol, however, weaving together a tapestry from very different strands and creating a pattern not at all as simple as it might at first appear.

From colonial days to the present, the welcome extended to any who have sought to enter the society has usually been genuine, if occasionally grudging, and frequently based on perceived self-interest. For example, Massachusetts Bay did not hang Quakers after the 1660s. But this toleration was not because the colony had developed a policy of actively welcoming them! Rather, the costs, both internal and external (repression at home and political conflict with England), of maintaining a policy of excluding the troublesome Quakers in order to preserve and maintain a rigorous religious establishment were perceived as too great to bear. In the simplest sense the open door policy can be understood in terms of benefits accruing to American interests: the crudest expression entailed the importation of cheap labor as a commodity, allowing no relationship between the exploited and existing communities in the society. There has unquestionably been a procession of small and large groups entering American life essentially to provide the human resources to make possible relentless economic growth. The role began with slaves from Africa and indentured servants from England, then swelled to include large groups of central and eastern Europeans, small contingents of orientals, and, more recently, Spanish-speaking groups and Southeast Asian refugees. In this respect the receptivity of the new homeland has been little more than potential for exploitation by American self-interest.

In terms of cultural self-understanding, however, one may see a more positive aspect to American toleration for immigrant groups. In this broader construction, the meaning has centered less on toleration (which at best thinly veils contempt) and more on a significant openness to others. This more positive perspective has also been present from the outset of American culture as, for instance, a genuine welcoming of certain peoples—a fine example being the experience of Jews in the American colonial society. These wanderers across the globe seemed to offer a direct contact with the Bible, which was so influential in the Puritan self-understanding. Although it certainly produced strains and conflicts, the ethnic mixture of the middle colonies also represented a readiness on the part of the Dutch, the Germans, the Scotch-Irish, the English, the Swedes, and an assortment of other individuals and groups to co-exist and possibly to intermingle with others. This receptivity continued to be a part of American self-understanding through the subsequent centuries, leading to such notable episodes as the shelter provided the generation of European intellectuals which fled fascist persecution.[22] In this broader sense, the operative ideal of the society has been a cosmopolitanism.

A third and rather more mythic aspect of this perspective can be identified: the highly idealistic vision or construction of American society which occasions the transformation of those who enter it into a "new humanity." The image was expressed in literary form in the well-known question of Crèvecoeur's as he reflected about the new republic: What is the American, this new man?[23] It can probably be traced back to sixteenth and seventeenth century speculations about the new-found continent and transformative powers associated with it. Assumptions about the generative and regenerative powers of American social life nourish this mythic construction. Fullest expression is given to it in Emma Lazarus' sentimental phrases, "Give me your tired, your poor, your huddled masses yearning to breathe free."[24] In strictly imagistic terms, this idea is represented by the melting pot. It has been variously conceived. At one extreme it appealed to Henry Ford in a literal sense, while for sociologically inclined students of American society it has been an analytical model.[25]

This latter mythic element, which highlights America's regenerative capability, represents powerful currents in American life. Typically, America's receptivity was most strongly expressed by those who viewed this society as the land of promise or among those who dramatically "made it," often overcoming what seemed to be insurmountable odds. A poignant protrayal of this meaning has been given in the fine film, "The Emigrants," which touchingly portrays the common people's excitement at the prospect of moving from the old homeland to the "land of promise." That vast numbers of emigrants should have left European lands at the height of the period of modern nationalism indicates the depth with which this idea of America as a new homeland penetrated the consciousness of common people in Europe.[26] It does not matter that this symbol—America's accessibility as a land of promise—was merchandised by salesmen. (From this point of view, Mormon missionaries and entrepreneurs of shipping lines performed much the same function.) The depth of resonance —the important point—is clear.

"America as the home for the homeless," "America opening arms for masses yearning to be free"—these sentiments seem of questionable validity in the later years of the twentieth century and may seem empty in our time. But in the interpretation of American culture the significance of this complex of images runs deep and must be part of any analysis giving serious attention to the religious set of meanings which has defined American experience. The symbol of receptivity comes to us out of the past. It may be tarnished in the present and clearly has a diminished currency. Thus, there is a temptation to overlook it. To assume that this perspective has lost its power is hazardous, however, since in the shifting kaleidescope of American social life old elements reappear in new patterns. The image of America's being open to the world's oppressed, for example, played relatively little role in making intelligible the society's participation in the World War II. After the war, however, it became a controlling symbol and contributed to the rather extraordinary dedication of resources to the rebuilding of Europe and the extension of assistance to newer nations. In analyzing the meaning of America's receptivity, we must certainly recognize how idealistic aspects have been continuous with those proceeding from the crassest self-interest. Currently this strand of religious meaning is not ascendant within the constellation of social commitments. But it does remain in the fabric of the received American culture, and its importance in the past must not be underestimated.

A fourth constituent symbol with pronounced religious content comes out of American social experience and is fundamental to its culture. This is the assumption that the society represents opportunity to its members, especially as individuals. This complex meaning is composed of many separate elements. One such thread is the ideal of political liberty, which is spun out in the eighteenth century as prelude to the struggle for independence. (Of course genetically it can be traced back into English Whig thought).[27] Economic enterprise and the protection of entrepreneurialism is also elaborated in both individual and collective versions, especially in the years following the Civil War.[28] Another element is the possibility of social liberty which develops rather later as the collective implications of particular natural rights are explored. Thus America as the land of opportunity is a construction that serves to legitimate widely varying patterns of individual initiative while supporting the tradition of limited government. In the extreme it works to circumscribe the elementary powers of government to regulate, investigate, or prohibit for the good of the whole society.

At least since de Tocqueville's analysis was offered,

students of American culture have identified liberty as a central, perhaps *the* central social symbol characteristic of American culture. But few students have been as successful as de Tocqueville in charting the ways in which the idea of liberty has set the style of individual life in the society, as well as the ramifications of the commitment to it in virtually all aspects of collective life. The individualistic component is so obvious and taken for granted that numerous commentators propose it as the primary root meaning of American life. This interpretation is all the more compelling in a framework of analysis which emphasizes individual self-consciousness to the exclusion of collective or corporate aspects of the question. But the basic goal in the present study is delineation of collective or corporate religious aspects of American society. From this point of view, individualism and individual liberty is a partial if not a false consciousness which must be explored in relation to social reality. Whatever content there is to individual liberty, social or collective forces provide the context or setting. It is in this sense that individual liberty as a social symbol must be interpreted against the reality of American society. We can illustrate how in its religious meaning liberty assumes particular shape.

In terms of social symbols our semi-mythic cultural heroes, from Daniel Boone to Howard Hughes, are perceived as rugged individualists suitable for emulation. Further reflection will suggest that this perception is based on systematically veiling how individuals relate to the social constraints we know to be mundane reality. For example, we now know that Howard Hughes had no existence apart from the shadowy Summa Corporation whose literal prisoner he was. In a similar way, other symbols of individualism mask from us the collective dimensions or social dependencies of our culture. Of course in any case the true individuality, of which Erich Fromm wrote, is probably too great a burden for most humans to shoulder.[29] (This society has escaped, through accidents and good fortune, the fascist or collectivist outcomes of disillusionment which European lands experienced in the 1930s.) But the interesting point is how in the American setting various strategies have been created in the society to make it seem as if the myth represents reality. One strategy is that the ideal of individual opportunity is set in the context of other basic meanings (such as those discussed above), which work to *modify* its more extreme interpretations. As an example, individualism is modified through linkage to social ideals, like the notion of the millennium. Thus, the individualism tends to be muted by cultural context; the exploitative baron is celebrated for his philanthropy, the industrial tycoon by his service to the republic. There is, however, one consistent and important implication to this modification of the ideal of individualism: a deep tendency to perceive American life as fulfilled in plenty or abundance.[30] American culture has very little spiritual asceticism, even though in cross-cultural perspectives that is one classical means of exercising individual liberty.

These four basic meanings are embodied in and expressed through American culture. In different combinations they are part of our ordinary experiences in the media or our personal lives. These sets of symbols enable us to interpret our experience to ourselves. The four are not proposed as if they *exhausted* the set or the cluster of operative frameworks which might be identified as basic meanings of American social life. It would certainly be possible to sort out these strands in different ways. Additional clusters of ideas could be explored in great detail. These four particular rubrics have been selected because each has received attention through the years in scholarly writing about the American character. Each is also conventionally taken for granted in current journalistic analysis. They are basic to American self-understanding, as it is presented in popular culture. They are recognizable, and it is self-evident that even if as a matter of critical judgment they are false values, they have been important in the life of the society. They have provided a kind of meaning which is properly considered religious because they have established horizons of collective self-understanding and provided enduring motivations for individual and group life.

This approach to the understanding of religious meaning within American culture has been adopted to establish a rather important theoretical point. Discussions of religious aspects of the society have generally resolved into proposals that *a particular meaning* is at the center of the American life. For Sidney Mead, who has made numerous contributions to this discussion, the meaning of American life is located in a "Religion of the Republic," identified as a particular religious tradition shaped by the Enlightenment. In his interpretation this cultural event is thought to have been a philosophical revolution. As a result of it, human life in both narrower individualistic and more extensive national, global, and cosmic frameworks may now be interpreted in highly rational terms. By contrast, for Robert Bellah the meaning of the American Civil Religion is to bring the United States to recognize the crucial role it must play at a juncture of human history as the twentieth century closes. To avoid catastrophe and destruction, national particularism must be replaced by a universalism, and national self-interest must be transformed into global self-consciousness. Additional proposals about the religious meaning of American society have been as selective and, in most cases, as focused upon a single expectation or goal.

The discussion in this chapter has suggested that if it cannot be established that there is a particular closed set of beliefs at the center of a manifest religion of the society, it may be proposed that there is, nonetheless, an open set or cluster of meanings central to American culture. The particular symbols in this set are numerous, to some extent they are diffuse, and certainly they repeatedly undergo transformations. But the overall set is identifiably American, and the Americanness lies in the constellation more than in the separate elements.[31] The constituent meanings are not exclusively associated with American culture, but the overall set of meanings probably is. Furthermore, this kind of approach to the religious understanding of American culture makes it possible to deal with the empirical observation that there are sub-cultures, or particular combinations of the meanings. A sub-set has intense reality for a particular segment of the society, while other sub-sets have significance for other groups. If the religious meaning of the American society is not single, it may nonetheless be interpreted as pluriform within the culture and specific to it. This is to propose that American social life in its religious aspect must be conceived as manifold. Certainly it is as pluriform as the culture. It is probably more internally complex in its religious aspect than in its political, and definitely more pluriform than in its economic aspect. The religious perspective must be included as basic to understanding the unities as well as the diversities of the culture, and requires at least as much attention and competent analysis as the other perspectives more frequently discussed.

Review of the elements of meaning or symbols in the

culture which contribute to the religious framework of the society leads to a conclusion: American culture experienced in its religious aspect from within the society is pluriform. This does not mean that when viewed as a meaning system public religion in American history is shapeless or without coherence. It does mean public religion seems not to be narrowly focused or sharply restricted. Like the patterns of belief and behavior we have already reviewed, the patterns of meaning are diffuse. For this reason we must direct attention to the question of the institutional locations of public religion.

Chapter 6

SOCIAL INSTITUTIONS
AND AMERICAN PUBLIC RELIGION

In an early and reflective response to Robert Bellah's essay "Civil Religion in America," Philip E. Hammond praised the piece, "accepting . . . the essential correctness of [its] argument."[1] At the same time, Hammond offered some comments not intended to be, as he put it, in the form of "revisions of a thesis, but extensions." The original piece, he thought, represented a *"cultural* analysis" of the first order. "That is, he [Bellah] identifies a set of ideas, demonstrates their interrelatedness, and illustrates their appearance in American life." What was missing, he thought, was "the parallel structural analysis"—that is, attention to "the social structures through which this 'culture' lives."

It is axiomatic that for any ideas (and certainly religious ideas) to exist, there must be social positions, expectations, institutions, even laws for the origin, preservation, transmission, and revision of those ideas.[2]

Hammond's discussion brings into focus an extremely important issue. If patterns of belief and behavior, and frameworks of meaning are to be interpreted as elements of American public religion, then close attention must be directed to the question: What institutions support, indeed embody and serve as the instruments to maintain, this culture? It may be that in a less differentiated society—let us hypothesize one based on unwritten but nonetheless codified traditions—something like a religion would be identified as a cultural reality, although to the proverbial external observer it might appear wholly diffused and lacking any direct structure in the society. That religion might well be ubiquitous, certainly coextensive and in some sense identical with the culture. Perhaps it should be interpreted as the substance of the culture, or certainly as the whole culture viewed in a certain aspect. But if we are to review religious aspects of culture in a modern differentiated society, some closer attention must be given to particular institutional structures. This is especially the case when we are interested in a hypothesized public religion in American culture. Hammond's point therefore should be recognized not only as an appreciative comment on the original proposal that there is in American culture a specific civil religion, but also as the identification of a critical issue in the serious analysis of public religion. The structural question raised by Hammond is of primary importance. Searching review of this issue is a necessary condition for advancing discussion of public religion in America.

Hammond thought that the structural analysis ought to take particular directions. After raising an essentially rhetorical question—"What might be such social structures in the case of America's civil religion?"—he sketched some answers. Certainly explicit religious institutions—churches and comparable organizations—are obvious structures.[3] Beyond that group, the public education complex can be viewed as significant. On the one hand the institution of the public school is linked directly to government, and on the other it is central to a complex process: the socialization of succeeding generations.[4] Hammond suggested that the American legal tradition should also be viewed in the perspective of the civil religion question, since it is "vital in orchestrating the inevitable conflicts" in a pluralistic society.[5] In appreciatively responding to these comments and suggestions, Robert Bellah indicated that he found them "extremely attractive," praising them for avoiding the usual "definitional hassles" and for providing "a glimpse of functioning social reality."[6]

Without doubt, the question raised by Hammond provokes serious reflection on a basic issue, and the proposals he makes by way of sketching out the lines of possible analysis are highly suggestive. But it is interesting that this line of inquiry appears not to have been pursued vigorously in the interim. Perhaps the reason is that when the relevant materials in American society are approached with this particular question in mind, they appear to be ambiguous. Just as when comparable consideration is given to patterns of behavior and belief, and frameworks of meaning in the society, a "hard construction" of the religious characteristics of institutions does violence to the materials and forces the interpretation of them. This suggests that, with respect to the institutional aspect as well as the others, it is problematical to argue that there is a clearly defined civil religion in American culture. If that position does not directly warrant, it certainly skirts the edge of deserving, the judgment that it is an instance of reification. But this is to anticipate a conclusion which should follow rather than precede the present chapter. The procedure will be to review the kinds of institutions in American society which may be thought to support structurally public religion as a vital social movement in the culture.

In his comments Hammond noted that the American Way of Life that Herberg posited (that value complex which constituted the central spiritual structure of the society) was celebrated in and supported by the churches and other religious organizations, Catholic and Jewish as well as Protestant.[7] There are at least two dimensions to this position which should be recognized as separate although finally interrelated. One dimension is a more or less explicit, and certainly an indiscriminate, appropriation of symbols and ceremonies having primary reference to the American polity in the on-going elaboration of the major religious traditions in the society. This dimension also includes implicit cooperation between religious institutions and governments so that in a variety of ways the one becomes agent for the other and the line of demarcation between them is increasingly obscured. There are many examples common in everyday life: the display of the American flag in church sanctuaries, the reading or the acknowledgment of a Presidential Proclamation (for example, proclaiming Thanksgiving Day), prayers for public figures, acceptance of religiously performed marriage ceremonies in lieu of civil services, maintenance of chaplains in the military service and in Congress, preferential tax-treatment of religiously owned properties and donations to religious organizations (so much so that the question of their profitability and/or political neutrality is frequently at issue), and forms of the definition given to conscientious objection as interpreted in American law. A complete list of these explicit connections between religious institutions (especially the more ancient, traditional, and established) and civil society in America is impressively extensive. So much is this the case that it seems to provide a compelling argument that a religious culture like Herberg's American Way of Life finds institutional embodiment in the more explicit teachings and practices of the religious bodies in the society.

This argument is advanced even further by recognizing

that another dimension of the relationship also exists. This second dimension is more implicit than explicit, and it concerns questions of style more than matters of substance or practice. Here an exceedingly subtle point concerns the coloration assumed by the various religious institutions in American society. We need only indicate certain general insights implied in this perspective. The institutional form taken by religious bodies in the United States, for example, is characteristically American. Generally, churches are at once formally associations (*gesellschaft*), while they also predicate close ties to community groups (*gemeinschaft*) as well. While they are defined partly in geographical terms, their composition directly reflects class, ethnic, and status factors. These are not dichotomous categories, and the last set is probably the most basic and inclusive. In a deep and pervasive sense, the religious institutions of American society embody basic lines of division within the society as accurately as any other formality under which social divisions are expressed. The churches and religious groups are the expression of cultural pluralism in America.[8] Further, the coloration extends to such matters as the place and role of the religious professional, and the status and power of the laity in the American setting. Reflect for a moment on how deeply Americanized the rabbinate as a religious office has become. We should note both the changes in rabbinical practices and the changed place of the office within the tradition. (The rabbi is no longer the exemplar of learning in the Talmudic tradition so much as the chief organizer within the community and its representative to outsiders.) In one perspective, the far-reaching and precipitate institutional changes in the Roman Catholic Church in the United States in the course of the last decades can be interpreted as a function of the Second Vatican Council, and thus part of a general deromanization which has proceeded in the Church at large. (The list of major changes includes fundamental alterations in the pattern of vocations, searching revisions of the assumptions undergirding the office of the priest, and complementary changes in the understanding of the laity, which has now emerged a quite new sense.) The changes are also evidence of a basic Americanization, a bringing into line in a striking fashion of Roman Catholic ecclesiastical practices with those which have come to prevail in the Protestant communions and in the Jewish community.[9] Comparable patterns are also to be found in the range of alternate religious groupings in the society.[10]

At least in terms of an analytical framework, there have been these two dimensions of Americanization of the traditional religious institutions of the society. Two comments are called for. First, it is not at all clear that within an essentially vital society, a religious tradition can preserve itself and avoid contamination from the culture of the society. The Amish represent a central case in point of the attempt to do just that within American social life.[11] Although the central impulse remains present for the old order, the more interesting development is the differentiation of the community according to degress of accommodation to the world. Another example is provided by the Orthodox Jewish community located in the Williamsburg section of Brooklyn.[12] Pursuing the same cultural strategy as the Amish, but over a much shorter time, there would already seem to be some evidence for beginnings of acculturation. Perhaps only in the setting of a rapidly declining central society can the religious strategy of isolation and avoidance of contamination prevail.[13]

The second comment is that thoroughgoing evidence for the Americanization of traditional religious institutions in the United States does not necessarily prove to be evidence that a differentiated American public religion is primarily expressed in and through them. Conceptual clarity is required at this point. If, for example, Will Herberg's American Way of Life is taken as the form of the American public religion, then the religious bodies we have discussed may provide the institutional locus for it "in, with, and under" the particular and separate religious traditions. If a more positive and differentiated civil religion is meant, however, then the role of the traditional religious bodies in expressing, supporting, and fostering religious particularism is directly at cross-purposes to their primary identities as religious institutions. It is important to insist that the institutionalization of public religion must accord with the *kind* of religion posited. The more manifest the religion is believed to be, the more explicit and exclusive the institutional expression required. Thus the existing religious institutions are more likely to provide structural support for a nonexclusive American public religion than for a differentiated positive version of it. This perception has led students of this question to look toward the public schools as that social institution in and through which an American public religion of a more explicit and differentiated type may be supported and sustained.

It is necessary to be clear about the implications of the proposal that the public schools institutionalize American public religion. The issue is not properly framed in a broad-gauged manner, in terms of the increasingly secular relationship between religion and education in American experience. This is subject worth serious study both as a large-scale transformation through time and in more limited cases. The long-term secularizing trend from colonial times to the present is a relevant, although finally remote consideration for the present inquiry. The purposes behind development of colonial education (preservation of a learned ministry, a literate laity, and so on) and the content of the education given ("In Adam's Fall we sinned all. . . .") were closely tied to particular Protestant traditions at the outset. This connection dissolved in the course of the nineteenth century, the content becoming nonsectarian and generalized though still largely Protestant Christian (Horace Mann), and finally evincing a neutral or even secular complexion in the twentieth century.[14] Particular episodes or incidents in the transitions are fascinating, for instance, the Cincinnati Bible struggle in the 1870s, and the parochial school issue of the 1920s.[15] The significant issue for the discussion at hand, however, lies still deeper, and requires precise analysis to receive proper definition.

What must concern us is the question: *Does* the public school system function as "the church"—or at least in a significant manner as a direct institutionalization of public religion in America?[16] If this is a more sharply focussed question in particular respects, it opens into a set of issues which are bewildering in their complexity. Some of the more striking ramifications are: (1) Is the requirement that all American youth complete public education or its equivalent to a certain point usefully interpreted as evidence that schooling basically entails initiation into full citizenship in the republic? (2) Are the schools mechanisms for a unique sort of socialization with respect to the culture, apart from other increasingly powerful mechanisms like television? (3) Is there a pronounced and identifiable latent agenda in the schools, as opposed to the formal and manifest curriculum, and does this agenda relate directly to the discussion of public religion? This kind of issue may be elaborated at great length. What is important for the purposes of this inquiry is less to complete the set of issues than to recognize the direction in which these issues develop.

The questions indicated above connect directly with the emotionally charged and on-going discussions of the schools as instruments of social control in American society. Recent literature has tended to be exceedingly critical of the schools, for in serving as instruments of social control, they have sacrificed the more individual results of education (enhancement of the ego, development of particular skills, reinforcement of creativity, and so on) to the perpetuation of the system, or the collective goal of social stability. The recent literature in this vein is legion.[17] In light of the kind of criticism there leveled against public education, the implication would seem to be that the schools function structurally to perpetuate the culture, finally appearing to be something very like an institutionalization of the religious elements of the culture.

Looked at in this light, it is important to see that the content of the curriculum matters less than the processes through which the institution establishes the real lessons to be learned. The encouragement of student government elaborately modeled on adult institutions, the valuing of conformity over originality, the stress placed upon behavior (including glorification of controlled violence through elaborate sports programs) are all powerful cultural elements in American society. Along such lines it is not far-fetched to argue that the public schools should be recognized as the Durkheimian church of the public religion in America.

But before we are swept away with enthusiasm for this construction, certain problems with it should be noted. First, other messages are also given out along with those previously noted. As a Church of the American Republic, the schools manifest many of the characteristics which seem to render the traditional churches of the society increasingly marginal to the social system. Local (congregational) autonomy expressed through boards of education (elders) and insufficient levels of funding (religious giving) have rendered professionals (clergy) rather impotent. Further, the status of these professionals and their institutions is understood to be (and will remain) comparatively low. The importance attached to public education in the operation of the market is dramatically evident. Traditionally, secondary education has been a profession for women. But the aggressive, aspiring, and liberated members of that sex now look to conquer the bastions of male supremacy—law, medicine, and business. While some males may be drawn into the primary and secondary levels of education, in the large they are viewed as men unqualified and unambitious enough to compete in other spheres. Alternatively, once a part of the system, they are generally siphoned off into supervisory or administrative positions. From the side of the structural-functional role of the schools, then, however promising the suggestion, the evidence about general attitudes and the insecure posture of the institution are sufficiently ambiguous to pose sharply critical questions if the case is seriously advanced.

Second, at the same time this case is subject to questions from the other side. For some decades, certain voices have called for the school to be seen as the Church of Democracy. Most explicitly, it has been held that democratic ideals provide the content, while democratic procedures supply the form, of sacralizing the American Way. Often the proposal entailed advocating a secular content for American education in order to achieve a unitary culture. This position was most clearly evident in the writings of John Dewey. For Horace Kallen, cultural pluralism came to represent, finally, an intolerable weakness in the society.[18]

On a more strictly institutional side, J. Paul Williams consistently worked through the implications of this position and staunchly advocated that the schools should not only be perceived, but self-consciously developed, as the temples of a democratic order.[19] What is interesting about this position is that when it is spelled out with full rigor and advanced as a social goal, *the actual reality* of American public education seems far from being in accord with it. What from the point of view of contemporary critics are their system-serving characteristics provide materials for a convincing case that the schools fall far short of constituting a church of a democratic society, let alone one for a differentiated and positive American civic cult.

At the most, therefore, it seems proper to conclude that the schools of the society are *among* those institutions that may function to sustain public religion as an aspect of American culture. But this step serves to shift the subject into a slightly different focus. It joins with considerations reviewed in preceding chapters to make it more difficult to maintain the argument that a coherent civil religion is a positive religious tradition in the society. That same argument, however, does have the additional implication that we might find institutional embodiment, or structural-functional locations, of the public religion of American culture at several points in the social fabric. If the subject is turned in this way, it is possible that the institutions already discussed may contribute in different ways and in combination with others to the religious maintenance of the specific American culture. Traditional religious institutions and school systems joined with additional institutions function to elicit/induce patterns of behavior and belief, and frameworks of meaning. These patterns may be organized in such a way as to maintain and propagate public religious reference. A thoroughly diffused institutional base of this kind does imply that the public religion of long-term consequence in American society has not been highly differentiated. This also means there is no compelling evidence for and institutional basis in the society for a sharply differentiated and explicit civic cult.

In his commentary, Hammond went on to suggest that in American society the law might be perceived as having sacred functions, especially in establishing acceptable behavior within the society. To some extent, it might also contribute to the proper interpretation of belief and prove to be a carrier of social meaning. Hammond's development of this point started with the observation that natural rights were a central tenet in the tradition of public religion (for example, as explicitly espoused in the Declaration of Independence). As a consequence, jurisprudence as the determination of these rights and their application to cases serves to make the legal institutions of the society carriers of public religion in a direct and immediate fashion.[20] Obviously, the connection thus suggested is an important element in the American social fabric. It needs to be qualified, however, by recognizing that the case law tradition, so deeply ingrained in the character of the American system, elaborates political rights under the Constitution as the charter of the government, rather than deriving them from the natural rights formulation standing behind the Declaration of Independence. In the case law tradition, the law is far less sacrosanct than in a natural rights formulation, and the jurists far less remote and god-like. Indeed, we intuitively recognize that the American legal tradition is closely tied to the political matrix of the society. So much is this the case that we conventionally identify it as a branch of the government.

If it is not a convincing argument that natural rights as elaborated and applied through jurisprudence is an expression of American public religion, however, there is another sense in which the legal institutions and traditions may turn out to provide structural support for religious aspects of the culture. In its substance this is the maintenance of boundaries, the setting of limits, beyond which behaviors and beliefs will not be tolerated within the social order. Like the case of the churches and religious institutions, this is separable into at least two dimensions. First, the law establishes limits explicitly by directly defining particular patterns of behavior and belief that will not be permitted. The best example for our purposes is probably the progressive refinement in the courts of the definition of conscientious objection, doing so by analogy to the theological position adopted by informed religious traditions of the society. This suggests that in order for symbols to be viewed, so to speak, as religious beliefs and symbols *before the law*, they shall resemble in form, if they do not have a comparable content, elements of Judeo-Christian faiths. Thus the latter in some sense become archtypal for religions in the society. Less explicit examples could also be explored through which American law (as case law, which operates as precedential) determines the forms, the social beliefs, and the boundaries of behavior, thus providing an operational locus of public religion.

There is another means through which the American legal system implicitly connects with the question of ways public religion may be institutionalized in the society. This is through defining the general boundaries of life in terms of the social roles and relationships tolerated in America. Of course the boundaries are indicated by the limits beyond which deviance is not permitted, which simultaneously signals what is permissible. In this sense, the law marks out more explicitly than any other aspect of the

American social system the range of life styles appropriate to and acceptable in the American culture. In a less thoroughly differentiated culture, these concerns might be more explicitly religious—that is to say, explained through a reference framework codified in terms of religious language. The colonial period of American history gives good examples of this, indeed has provided materials for a systematic analysis of how this works.[21] Early modern European societies generally struggled over these issues in terms of religious worldviews. In this sense the relative absence of explicit public religious reference in the legal system as it operates in this society further calls into question, it would seem, the hypothesis that there is a differentiated American civic cult. There is no question that functional equivalents to the boundary-setting which takes place in more manifestly religious societies exist in the social roles of American law.

The initial sections of this chapter have explored the comments Philip Hammond made about Robert Bellah's essay. By elaborating positions he suggested, we have canvassed important possibilities generally overlooked in discussions of American public religion to date. The overall trend of the analysis has been toward an increasingly sceptical position. On the basis of a structural analysis of American society, it does not appear that there is strong evidence for the existence of a differentiated public religion. The trend of this discussion has been toward accepting an understanding of civic piety as more diffused. It may be, however, that additional relevant structural elements should be identified in the society. For if religion of the public realm in America is diffused, then the social structures fostering civic piety should be located among a variety of social institutions. In addition to the particular social structures already reviewed, at least two other institutional locations seem to be significant.

One is the communications industry, which engulfs citizens with specific messages and provides the generalized content for our individual and collective lives. For numerous reasons the place of the media in American society seems to receive far less attention as a *serious* topic than is warranted. Some of these reasons are obvious. Intellectuals, or those who view themselves as intellectuals, generally associate culture with high culture, particularly the culture of the stage and the printed page. The popular culture of the *hoi polloi*, by contrast, is assumed to be unworthy of serious attention. Further, the research effort of that social science which is directed to the study of human cultures—anthropology—has, at least until recently, focussed on the remote and the isolable (in terms of location, scale, and complexity) rather than the near and the overwhelming. In addition, among many reflective students of American life, there is a kind of bias against interpreting as significant any aspect of culture associated with filthy lucre, and the communications business in modern America, especially commercial television, does not conceal the intimacy of the relationship. Can any piety be taken seriously which has such an exceedingly blatant relationship to profit? A further consideration is the basically Puritan-Victorian attitude towards diversion and entertainment as not serious; an industry devoted to merchandizing such products systematically challenges that vigorous single-mindedness with which productive pursuits (work) are to be addressed. Thus modern American popular culture, including magazines with extensive circulations and the press as well as television, does not *appear* to merit reflective attention as a location for serious study of public religion.

Yet it is evident that in the course of the last century a *national* culture, in the technical sense of the term, has been coming into existence. This culture is so pervasive and powerful that only eccentric individuals and groups, or communities firmly committed to alternative styles of life maintain much distance from the influence of mass communication. (Examples of the latter include some communities which are archaic, like the Orthodox Jews of Williamsburg or the Old Order Amish, and some contemporary utopian communities which explicitly resist modernity.) The communications industry facilitates interaction within the society, thus holding it together. It also influences, not to say manipulates, consumer tastes and preferences, and increasingly structures the use of leisure time. The national television networks are the great contemporary engines of this culture, having developed from recent technological inventions, but they stand in a line of innovations which have relentlessly worked to transform culture. Certainly the spread of the telegraph and the telephone began the modern stages of this development (followed closely by movies and radio). Concurrently, the popular press created publications (tabloids, cheap magazines, and so on) which appear to be independent, but actually serve a complementary function. *TV Guide* is the most rational example of a far more general integration of the several modes of popular culture into a general one which, while it may appear to be internally differentiated, is actually not so at all with respect to public religion. The mediums of print, sound, and sight are all connected and orchestrated so that the effective impact upon social values, including patterns of belief and behavior as well as meanings, is comprehensive.

An earlier comment suggested that leisure activities are closely tied to the development of the communications industry. It is not accidental that professional sports have exploded in just the same period of time. Professional athletics is so perfectly suited to the needs of the media that if it hadn't happened, it would have had to be invented. In fact, of course, it was invented to fill a new pattern of cultural space and time created by the communications industry. Through newspaper, radio, and television, the world of sports has become central to American popular culture. This content of the culture has been delayed in development, or retarded and forced from center stage, so to speak, only by periods of national warfare in which the teams and players were simply different, and the contests played according to rules with more deadly import. But the reporting of the events was remarkably similar, and the response of heightened patriotism has been scarcely distinguishable from the intense loyalty to the favorite team. While William James remarked upon the role of athletics as the "moral equivalent for war," in terms of the content of culture, war has been the only "religious equivalent for sports." All of this commitment to athletic performance can be seen at one level as a fundamental dramatization of the basic values and goals of the society. The emphasis upon success, closely identified with money, derived from brute power melded with technical expertise, is perhaps the most direct and telling dramatization of the content of the American culture developed in the last century. When the modern communications business is not directly merchandizing sports, that culture is evoked indirectly through virtually exclusive attention to the same themes of controlled violence, exhancement of skills, and celebration of victory. Much of the humor in the media is derived from associating the viewer with the victim and making fun of the latter's plight, indirectly if not directly.

But if this culture created and sustained through the modern means is linked to public religion in America in the manner suggested, it is still not evidence for a differentiated civic cult. Rather, and this brief review confirms the conclusions emerging from the preceding analysis of social institutions, the civic piety of the culture does not transcend American life, is thoroughly conventional in its values, and certainly is not differentiated from other aspects of culture in the manner suggested by Hammond. Thus, we are brought to a position with respect to the communications industry and the sports-culture of the society not far removed from the conclusions we have reached in reviewing other social institutions.

An additional institutional expression of public religion in America may be identified. Interestingly enough, it may be closer to a church, or series of denominations of civic piety, than those already considered. The status of these institutions is basically marginal to the society, perhaps increasingly so, and the influence they exercise is extremely episodic and accidental, although not by any means negligible. The status of these institutions within the culture does further erode the judgment that we may confidently delineate a differentiated religion of the public realm.

The American civic piety is given its most direct institutional and organizational expression through both more and less explicitly patriotic voluntary societies and lodges. One of the more interesting aspects of this suggestion is the relative lack of attention given to the range of phenomena in question. Of course, nativist movements (the American Protective Association or the Ku Klux Klan) have been repeatedly analyzed in context, and passing mention has been made in studies of American society of the political importance of such organizations as the American Legion and the Veterans of Foreign Wars. In addition to humorous allusions, such groups as the Daughters of the American Revolution and the scouting organizations have been noted as important voluntary associations in the society. But almost without exception, attention has been given to particular organizations rather than to the complex as a whole. The staggering dimensions of that complex have eluded serious discussion, and little systematic analysis has been undertaken with respect to the cultural significance of the phenomenon. Certainly the structural/functional place of this complex has not been studied in relation to the question of public religion in American society.

While initially it may seem inappropriate to look at this complex as a possible institutional locus for American civic piety, some reflection should suffice to clarify the issue. It does not seem strange to us that common linguistic usage refers to the Christian Church or the Jewish tradition in American society, even though the number of Christian denominations is extraordinary, and the range of practices and beliefs in the Jewish community is great. No more should we assume, by analogy, that there must be a single coherent organization, or one institution only, through which the American public religion might receive social expression. Religious pluralism in America has made voluntaryism the framework within which all religious belief and behavior is asserted. That may as well be true for American civic piety as for developed traditions with ancient roots or modern innovative movements. As within the set of Christian denominations, there are clusters or groups which reflect similar kinds of origins and have distinct correlations with social locations (class, region, status, as well as other accidental conditions). Accordingly, we might surmise that the complex of voluntary organizations sustaining American civil religion would be at once manifold and interrelated. Indeed, we might expect to find networks within the overall complex corresponding in some measure, let us say, to the National Association of

Evangelicals, the American Catholic Welfare Conference, the National Council of Churches, and the American Jewish Congress. On reflection, this characteristically American kind of institutional development is exactly what we should expect to find as the institutional form of American public religion, if the proposal is to be taken with analytic seriousness. What is astonishing is the lack of rigorous attention to the conceptual issue and the virtual absence of concern with this panoply of groups.

Voluntary or associational activity represents an extraordinarily pervasive condition of collective life in American society. This is to say that numerous societies and agencies are extremely important in creating and sustaining the American social fabric. Americans have built up their collective life and finally governed themselves to quite a remarkable degree in this way. A. M. Schlesinger, Sr., offered a descriptive analysis of this phenomenon in his "Biography of a Nation of Joiners."[22] While from time to time this perspective has been used in the study of a particular episode (nativist groups) or an epoch (the "Burned-Over District"), on the whole it has not been systematically elaborated as a perspective on American society. Most certainly this approach has not been utilized to illuminate its cultural aspects.[23] From this point of view, American religious life must generally be interpreted as a sub-set of the voluntary associational life of the society. This particular sub-set has especially close links to ethnic traditions, to countries of origin, to race, and to class-based differentiation of the society. Religious life is also closely linked to family structures, perhaps even more so than other kinds of voluntary groups which may make much less of the family and the transmission of values between generations. Especially through groups like the Catholic Youth Organization, the Young Mens and Young Womens

Christian Associations, and the Jewish equivalents, the religious communities are closely linked to another sub-set of voluntary groups much more directly oriented to the control of government. They are especially concerned with patriotism and loyalty to the nation (not of course to the exclusion of self-interest shared among members). Exclusively male groups of this sub-set such as the American Legion have frequently been augmented with auxiliary groups for females so that the sub-set is more inclusive than might at first appear.[24]

Included in the patriotic sub-set are at least the following kinds of organizations. First, *veterans organizations*, a kind of group begun in the United States after the war for Independence as "The Society of the Cincinnati" (1783). The modern pattern was laid down, however, in the development of the Grand Army of the Republic after the Civil War (1866). Subsequent wars have led to the founding of comparable social organizations for their veterans. The most active at the present time are the American Legion (1919) and the Veterans of Foreign Wars (1913). Second, *hereditary organizations* in which the defining characteristic may be connection with colonial stock, for example, or with the revolutionary struggle. A parallel structure is provided in ethnic groups (for example, Italian-American Clubs). Third, more strictly *fraternal orders* like the Masonic Lodges, the Elks, Rotary, which, at least in some respects, are to be seen as celebrating the new free American society in which unregulated associations permitted the unhindered development of group life. Fourth, basically *scouting groups* in which there is provision for the socialization of the younger generation into patterns of belief and behavior rather heavily defined by patriotism and loyalty to traditional values. Finally, at least certain of the broadly *nativist groups*, of which some are aggressively hostile to immigrants as well as others more moderate in tone. A small and generally evanescent sub-set is composed of groups which have developed in response to perceived threats to America, the most recent concerned with bolshevism and communism in the middle decades of the twentieth century.[25]

By thus indicating the range of voluntary groups within this broad category, our intent is not to maintain either explicit and acknowledged or implicit and unacknowledged identity between them. Rather, it is to make clear what a broad and influential number of associations in American society serve to provide religious identification within the society. Further, their latent if not manifest content basically orients members toward issues of civic behavior, belief, and meaning, whatever other functions they may serve. Each of the groups has its own version of American beliefs, has developed its characteristic ritual behaviors to act out the kind of loyalty perceived as appropriate to American society, and attributes a special cluster of meanings to the nation. What is common to all is the sense that this society is the sacred collectivity deserving final loyalty. Sacrifices for it have been made, and must be made in the future, if required.

This is the sense in which under a structural/functional analysis, given the conditions of voluntaryism in religious life generally, this large set of associations ought to be interpreted as an important institutional location of American public religion. It is remarkable how little attention has been devoted to this subject, possibly because civic piety and concern about public religion have typically been issues of moment for intellectuals who by personal inclination and social location are infrequently linked with this complex of associations in American life. It may also be that such a social location seems to reduce civil religion, or civic piety, to little more than patriotism. If that is the case, we should especially regret that something so obvious has been overlooked.

This species of associational behavior may be fruitfully analyzed in much the same way that other formal social movements are studied. One of the more useful frameworks recently proposed shifts attention from the more static formal structures of religious institutions to more dynamic characteristics of social movements. Gerlach and Hine have posited five key factors which operate to make movements possible:

1. *A segmented, usually polycephalous, cellular organization*
2. *Face to face recruitment* by committed individuals . . .
3. *Personal commitment* generated by an act or an experience which separates a convert . . . from the established order . . .
4. *An ideology* which codifies values and goals, provides a conceptual framework . . . , motivates . . . , defines the opposition, and forms the basis for . . . unification of a segmented network of groups
5. *Real or perceived opposition.* . . .[26]

Obviously the more directly self-interested and benign of the myriad associations fulfill these conditions less fully than do those that are more strident and aggressive. But this perspective on them does suggest kinds of parallelism that link seemingly unlikely pairs like the DAR and the KKK, or the Rainbow Girls and the American Legion. We should not expect that every citizen would necessarily be committed to American public religion, any more than the universalism of Christian language results in church membership approaching 100 percent of the community. Rather, in these associations there exist linguistic and behavioral communities oriented to the American society as a religious reality. Insofar as public witness is rendered, as on Memorial Day or the Fourth of July, the true believers symbolically display the roles they believe that they bear for the whole community throughout the year.

Because competing and perhaps exclusive final claims are made by many of these societies to interpret and guard the true American polity, tensions are present among them, and between them and the traditional religious denominations. (This kind of tension is not so obvious between the conventional denominations and the schools, the law, or the communications industry.) At times these relations are highly strained; at other times cooperation is possible. There is always the possibility for radical divergence between the associations as religious cults of the society and the formal religious bodies. Such divergence in terms of behavior, belief, and meaning is rooted in conflict between perceptions of collective interests.

This chapter has been an attempt to explore ways in which public religion may be institutionalized in American society. More exactly, it has pursued this inquiry, following Philip Hammond's lead, in terms of social analysis as a necessary complement to cultural analysis. The general conclusion is similar to that reached in the preceding chapters on religious belief, behavior, and meaning in the society. There is data which can be construed as evidence that there is a public religion. But the data seems far from establishing that there is an institutionalized civic cult. In this way the institutional evidence resists interpretation, finally appearing to be as opaque as the data with respect to beliefs, behaviors, and meanings. We are led to the conclusion that attention must be directed toward another question: What are the appropriate types of models, or concepts, through which we may advance interpretation of the data concerning public religion?

Chapter 7

THE INTERPRETATION OF PUBLIC RELIGION IN AMERICA

Throughout this study we have repeatedly encountered a basic issue in the interpretation of evidence, particularly evidence about collective patterns of behavior and belief. The issue is that in the most literal sense (as well as in more sophisticated senses), evidence is never free of interpretation. Initially, implicit assumptions select what is immediately perceived as well as what is registered and reported about any social fact. Additional filters influence the transmission of evidence—through unrecognized biases as well as manifest interests. Especially with respect to historical data, accidents deeply affect the process of transmission. Finally, at the point of interpretation for any given time, selectivity operates at many levels in both an interpreter and the various audiences for his work.

This generic problem of data and its interpretation has received particular attention in the natural sciences; it is also a given in the work of social scientists and humanists. Fundamentally, the problem cannot be solved or the conditions overcome. Established paradigms finally give way to a new organizing insight. Social scientific hypotheses must be repeatedly offered, and tested. Those that prove useful will be secure as credible theories; those that do not will be discarded. Historians as artful scientists will seek to enlarge the scope of their conventional bases of data, while attempting to interpret evidence in more intellectually

compelling ways through micro-level and macro-level constructs—whether or not they are conscious of so doing.

Optimally, one must combine critical reflection about
the precarious *condition* of all social knowledge with theoretically informed study of the appropriate data. The preceding chapters have aimed at this result, emphasizing
identification of the range and variety of data concerning
public religion in American life. This concluding chapter
turns to review the range of operative models through
which the phenomena might be interpreted in order both
to balance the discussion of the problem and to offer a
useful theoretical contribution as the discussion of this
topic proceeds. Our attention necessarily first turns to
Robert Bellah's formulation, especially as it was developed
in his initial essay on civil religion, but also as refined,
augmented and, qualified in subsequent articles and a
book.[1] Related conceptual proposals have been made by
others (both before and since Bellah introduced the specific
term). These have been aggregated so that civil religion
has become a generic designation for a significant number
of different proposals about the relationship between religion and society in modern America.[2] It will be productive
to attack the theoretical issues directly rather than to
review in detail the variety of relevant constructions which
have been developed in the last several decades. But initially the civil religion proposal itself will demonstrate how
mixed the models have been.

From the outset, at the center of the civil religion
discussion has been a basic ambiguity between what may
appear as apparently unrecognized shifts of meaning and
as intentional equivocation. Baldly stated, the question is
whether public religion is to be understood as a separate
and differentiated religion, identifiable by means of comparison with and contrast to other positive religious cults

in the society. Alternatively, it may be conceived as a dimension or aspect of the society which is present "in, with, and under" the whole, possibly including the specific religious traditions conventionally identified as such. This ambiguity is at the center of Robert Bellah's original essay. It is evident in the different formulations that are juxtaposed in the initial paragraph and at important points throughout the text. In the very first sentence of the essay, the author comments that "few have realized that there actually exists alongside of and rather clearly differentiated from the churches an elaborate and well-institutionalized civil religion in America."[3] This seems to be an unqualified assertion that there is a specific cult (properly identified as "American Civil Religion") which is understood as roughly comparable to other positive traditions of the society. But the second sentence, which concludes the paragraph and which might appear to be a parallel construction, includes a *caveat* that the careful reader will not overlook: "this religion—or perhaps better, this religious dimension—has its own seriousness and integrity and requires the same care in understanding that any other religion does."[4]

An unwary reader will interpret these sentences as parallel assertions which make the claim that civil religion in America is a positive religious tradition broadly comparable in an analytical perspective to the myriad other religions of the society—for instance, the American Lutheran Churches or the Roman Catholic Church in America. But a careful reader, noticing the preferred interpretation of it as constituting a "religious dimension," will recognize that a most significant theoretical point lies hidden under the discussion. The footnote to the paragraph addresses the issue of why attention had not been directed to "something so obvious" as American civil religion. Several reasons are adduced, including the fact that the subject is controversial (since some believe that Christianity is the national religion, whereas others interpret the separation of church and state as excluding that possibility). The most basic reason is the currency of a "peculiarly Western conception of 'religion,'" in which religion is viewed as having an exclusive claim on its subjects. Thus, "the Durkheimian notion that every group has a religious dimension . . . is foreign to us."[5]

The full implication of this theoretical position would seem to be not only that civil religion is a particular religious tradition in American society, but that civil religion is unique among American religions in its functions and characteristics. By definition it is the religious expression or manifestation of the American national life or the collective life of the whole society in a way that the more conventionally designated traditions are not. As such, it must be interpreted as a function of the coming to be or the achievement of a society in the American case which corresponds to the kinds of requisites Durkheim posited as necessarily entailed in every society.[6] Here there are some special considerations which must not be overlooked. For one thing, the absence in the American case of a traditional or feudal background, as Louis Hartz so compellingly argued, is a fundamental given.[7] In addition, the rapid and relentlessly increasing dependence upon industrial, bureaucratic and technological innovation in American society over the last century and a half constitutes a special set of conditions. Further, these developments were joined to a persisting cultural pluralism as a continental society emerged. These considerations *may* make it problematical to posit a fully developed American society in the manner necessary to satisfy the conditions implicit in Durkheim's analysis, at least until the Civil War.

The point which needs to be demonstrated is that in the American case there has been a religious dimension in the development of the whole society broadly comparable to that posited in other societies which have evolved according to rather different patterns.[8] If the religious dimension of American society has been manifested through the phenomena Bellah identifies, several questions remain. Has it constituted a "well-institutionalized civil religion," as he seems to suggest? And if it has, is the civil religion to be understood and interpreted as basically another religious tradition in the society? Alternatively, is it to be interpreted by virtue of its special function as a particular kind of cult—at least by comparison with other positive religions in a culturally pluralistic society?

The same ambiguity or equivocation emerges at a major transitional point in the essay when the author moves from discussion of the broad historical evidence for civil religion in America to comment about the phenomenon in the present—specifically, its current manifestations and the resources it might provide in the contemporary "time of crisis" in American life. Bellah explicitly acknowledges "reifying and giving a name to something that . . . has gone on only semiconsciously."[9] In justification of this move, he argues that others began the process of reification, but had done so as critics of "religion in general," the American Way of Life, or "American Shinto." He wished to balance the picture by suggesting the positive aspects of the tradition and by viewing it as a national, perhaps even global, cultural resource. To have reified the concept so explicitly, however, is to have shifted from a perspective in which the religious dimension of American life is interpreted as it is expressed through or institutionalized in particular ceremonies or symbols to one in which emphasis may appear to be placed upon the differentiation of a civic cult. In its reification it becomes a positive and independent religious tradition which then requires interpretation as one among other positive religious traditions, ancient and modern.

In this manner, Bellah's exceedingly stimulating and provocative essay seems to have embodied, or may even have been constructed upon, systematic ambiguity. One purpose of this monograph has been to sort out major strands of the discussion in order, at least, to identify if not to reduce the ambiguity. The thesis of the present chapter is that the shifts of meaning or the equivocations indicated above (which echo through the discussion of public religion) are produced by lack of clarity with respect to the claims made at the theoretical level. The ambiguity has been produced by the uncritically mixed modes of analysis and the confusion of models by different interpreters. (Indeed, it seems evident that the systematic ambiguity indicated above in part derives from the proposal advanced by Bellah himself.) That has made it more difficult to achieve clarity in discussion of the issue of public religion.

While helping to explain the fruitfulness of the proposal that there is an American civil religion, the shifts of meaning have actually worked to impede more fundamental analysis of the subject. Of course, the different meanings given to the term reflect divergent series of assumptions which have led to various constructions of the concept. Since in turn these frameworks determine the interpretation given to particular phenomena (so that the same evidence appears to be different in separate perspectives), additional clarity about the variety of frameworks is prerequisite to significant advance in discussion of the subject. It will be useful to identify four separate constructions of public religion in America. Each of them rests upon a distinctive set of premises, even rooting in separate intellectual traditions. Our purpose will be not to explore these traditions in detail, certainly not more than is necessary to indicate how distinguishable and often very different problematics underlie each one. It should be stressed that this undertaking is not an attempt to inventory all *possible* conceptions of public religion, or even all of the relevant concepts which have been proposed in the discussion to date. (Most operative concepts, like Bellah's, have actually turned out to be mixed models.) Analysis of this series of models should establish a different point—namely, that a range and variety of elements are present in current concepts. It should also give emphasis to the point that the issue of interpretation of evidence ramifies through discussions of public religion. This issue cannot be put aside or laid to rest, for assumptions are entailed at every step of the way and once made enter into the chain of evidence and interpretation.

One approach to operational concepts of public religion is to suggest that each roots in a specific philosophical and theoretical tradition, emphasizes a particular construction of relevant evidence, and is distinctive in terms of range, inclusiveness, and analytical penetration. For the purposes of this study, which has sought to advance a religious analysis of the material, it will be useful to order them in a continuum of religious representations. At issue is the religious referent—that is to say, the objects to which the relevant evidence (patterns of belief and behavior) have reference. Of course, other continuums of models might be proposed in terms of other aspects of the constructs. One option would be a continuum defined in terms of increasing institutional elaboration of public religion, while another might be an order based upon kinds of behaviors. Alternatively, the operational concepts might be reviewed in terms of their theoretical sources or their political utility. The decision to emphasize religious modes of representation is taken in order to place at the center of the discussion the world views which have manifest religious content rather than, for example, institutional or behavioral issues which are more explicitly political, however significant the latent religious implications.

It will facilitate the discussion to indicate the overall pattern of the continuum before giving attention to the operational concepts which comprise it. At one extreme is the position, classically developed by Durkheim, that each collectivity or social entity in the nature of the case is represented to itself as sacred. This is to hold that by definition every society has a religious dimension. On this view, American society, like any other, inevitably expresses an identity in religious terms. Durkheim's formulation was worked out primarily with reference to materials from relatively small and largely preliterate cultures. His work has proved to be a powerful resource, however, for many social theoreticians concerned with large, developed, and differentiated societies. In terms of our continuum, Durkheim's represents an extreme position since the collectivity itself is the sacred object, and, therefore, a religious dimension or aspect of social life exists without reference to the self-consciousness or intentionality of the members of the social group. Within this framework, the American nation has a life of its own, a religious life, without necessitating self-consciousness about it on the part of the individuals who comprise it and without necessary conflict between it and other differentiated religions. On this model, the collectivity is sacred and at the hands of an interpreter general symbolic behavior as well as specific ritual actions disclose the religious structure of the cosmos. This first model is a social model of public religion.

A second position along the continuum is less concerned

to identify the deep sources of religion within a society and more oriented toward analysis of the way in which a particular set of values functions in terms of interaction among the members of a given social order. The central analytical issue is the symbolic unity of the society in and through the action-guiding provisions which define the culture. This operational concept of public religion places less emphasis on ritual elements and symbol systems, looking instead to religious rituals and symbols as evidence for generally held values in or orientations to the society— patterns of behavior common to the culture, in some sense beyond review and criticism. On this model, religion is of no less concern to the whole society. Evidence for it, however, is located in terms of interactions within the social matrix. Sacrality is not necessarily attributed to the group, *per se*, for what counts as the object of religion is the culture which may have cosmic significance attached to it. The society is bearer of a culture which may be thought to have enduring significance. This second model might be termed a cultural model of public religion.

A third position along the continuum we have set out conceives public religion in terms of a particular political order. On this model society is not sacred and thus the object of religion, nor is culture viewed as endowed with religious significance. Here the presumed differentiation has proceeded to a further stage, and a particular political order (the Roman Empire, Nazi Germany, the American republic) is identified as requiring fundamental commitment and deserving final loyalty. This model may be construed in more instrumental terms—the commitment and loyalty are owed to a civil order which confers benefits. Under this construct, civic piety is a kind of rite of exchange erected on a very narrow base. Alternatively, it may entail a fuller elaboration, but will always emphasize the differentiated political order as locus for the appropriate religious practices. This model suggests why attention is repeatedly called to religious aspects of nationalism. We shall designate it the political model of public religion.

A final position on our continuum identifies the content of public religion with a separate realm. Here the specific religious interpretation is projected as a transcendent norm acting upon the political order, the general culture, and even the society (from which the others have been differentiated). Accordingly, this is a basically theological construction of public religion and little attention is given to rituals or symbolic behavior. Emphasis falls on beliefs and meanings which are thought to have existence independent of the society, its culture, and its politics. In the extreme case, a Biblical God appears before whom all else is relativized—except perhaps a chosen people who serve purposes attributed to Him. This will be termed a theological model for public religion.

The continuum so described is an essentially logical construct intended to call attention to the range of religious modes of representation which enter into discussion of public religion. As a related matter it should be noted that conceptualization of religion shifts as the move is made from one of the above models to another. Where the society as collectivity is sacred, the religious universe does not have room for a transcendent God. Conversely, when a transcendental divinity is postulated, society, culture, and also the political order are, from the viewpoint of the believer, relativized or desacralized in whole or in part. The religious constructs corresponding to the basic religious modes of representation will also vary in terms of symbolisms, associated behaviors, and beliefs. Of course, the matter of stipulated religious practice (piety) will also vary from one type of model to another.

Rather than pursue the question further at this abstract level (in terms of ideal types), it will be more useful to illustrate how very different constructions have been placed on the materials of public religion in America by interpretations broadly dependent upon these different kinds of theoretical sources. Of course, no empirical analysis conforms exclusively to one model in all particulars, especially an ideal-typical one. But several conclusions should be clearly established through this procedure. One is the significance of the variety of models in the interpretation of public religion, and the other is the different sets of data which are illuminated within these separate frameworks of analysis.

The model of public religion that posits society as a sacred object derives from the analysis developed by Emile Durkheim. In this framework every human collectivity or social grouping has a religious aspect, located in those sets of beliefs and "rites connected with them."[10] The beliefs and the ritual behavior establish the precise identity of the collectivity: "Wherever we observe the religious life, we find that it has a definite group as its foundation."[11] Indeed, so important is the religion to the group that the former may be said to have a reality through the collectivity over and beyond the reality it has for individuals. "They [the beliefs and rites] are not merely received individually by all the members of this group; they are something belonging to the group, and they make its unity."[12] From this point of view it is certainly the case that every religion expresses the basic identity of a group, and, conversely, so important is religion to the life of the group that no group is without its religion or religious dimension. This is very obvious in the case of primitive societies. Perhaps it is also evident in complex societies from which the observer has some distance. In any case, it was Durkheim's position that even if this truth (that every group has a religion) was less obvious with reference to developed and differentiated social orders (characteristic of the modern West), it held as a theoretical constant in any case. Religion is not to be identified as the beliefs and rituals of individuals or sub-groups. Its full reality is collective, and its object is the group as the most fundamental given in the world as socially determined. This truth may well be hidden from everyday perception, since it exists at or even below the threshold of conscious reflection. Furthermore, Durkheim insists that a religion necessarily is worked out in institutional expression: "In all history, we do not find a single religion without a Church."[13]

The relevance of such a set of premises to the interpretation of public religion in American society is obvious. First, it explains that public religion is the religious dimension of American life. Since it is presumed that no vital society can exist without it, and since America is presumed to be a functioning society, a religious expression of this collectivity as a social reality must exist. Therefore, on the basis of Durkheim's assumption, an American religion of the public realm is not only inevitable, it is critical to the life of the society. This explains why adherence to this cult has not been recognized for what it is. By definition, the religion of the collectivity belongs to the whole (the society) and not to the parts (the individuals), so that precisely while it is vital to the whole, it may nevertheless remain undetected by the members. Third, although expressed in and through institutions, it explains why evidence for public religion might appear in unlikely places and require interpretation.

It is obvious how deeply Robert Bellah's discussion of civil religion in America draws on the tradition of social thought about religion that goes back to Durkheim.[14]

Certainly one of his most significant points of departure from the premise that society itself is sacred is in the apparent belief that by something approaching self-conscious reaffirmation of the religion the group (American society) can be significantly reconstituted (pass through the third time of trial into a new period). A radically consistent Durkheimian perspective would question whether the collectivity had a continuing reality if its religious basis were so fully objectified. (In this sense the civil religion proposal has the form and feel of protestant revival or awakening conceptions.) There may be a better example available to us of how postulates derived from Durkheim have application to American materials. This is the work of W. Lloyd Warner, especially the concluding volume (the fifth) of his Yankee City series.

The Yankee City series was devoted to the detailed study of social systems in a multi-ethnic, religiously plural, industrialized, modern east coast city (Newburyport, Massachusetts). It concluded with a volume on the symbolic life of the community.[15] Sections of Warner's book, especially a segment devoted to analysis of Memorial Day observances, have been separately reprinted, and this material is repeatedly cited as evidence for the reality of civil religion in American social life.[16] Without calling into question the importance of this particular analysis, it is important to recognize that Warner seems to have viewed it as one among a host of symbol systems in the culture of Yankee City—and, by extension, American society. In addition, an explicit theory for interpretation of the data underlies it, including a distinction between technical, moral, and supernatural types of action context.[17] In this way Warner directly acknowledged the place of more strictly secular symbols (as well as explicitly sacred ones). Interestingly enough, the Memorial Day rites he analyzed, which have seemed to be such good evidence for civil religion, are classified by him as both secular and sacred. In a manner which indicates his theoretical dependence upon a Durkheimian framework, he argues it is possible to understand the life of the group only through its symbol systems. (The explicit differentiation of technical, moral, and supernatural symbols seems to introduce a basic qualification to Durkheim's position.)

What must be emphasized about Warner's materials is their richness and variety. In particular, he explores the symbolic aspects of political belief and behavior, especially as media coverage affects it (even before the advent of television coverage). In addition, his insight into the uses of social symbols within a community as counters in the struggle between class or status-based groups is telling. The position of the old families in Yankee City, he perceives, is maintained through political and economic power—which are scarcely separable from the manipulation of social symbols. Of course the identity of the community is spelled out in terms which link it to the broader contours of American history. For instance, the national community made demands upon Yankee City to which it responded, as in the Civil War and in the international crisis of World War I. Finally, generic human problems—birth, disease, death, the definition of good and evil, the relentless passage of time—receive symbolic structuring in Warner's view. In a strict sense, only the latter kinds of issues are a direct response to the supernatural and thus properly identified as religious. Religious questions in the public realm lie close to the political and moral issues. This consideration does not so much make these issues less religious as it serves to set them in a rich field of symbolic action. In turn, this renders suspect on theoretical grounds (among others) any attempt at clear-cut differentiation or separation of a civil religion from that far denser background. Taken as an approach, Warner's analysis of the symbolic life of Yankee City does not so much question the interpretation of particular symbols and associated behaviors such as Memorial Day Observances in public religious terms as it challenges at the conceptual level the proposal that civil religion is a discrete, differentiated, and developed religion in the society.

Interpretations of public religion which emphasize society itself as the sacred object derive from a Durkheimian understanding of religion. But the same analysis of symbolic process which is alleged to identify tangible evidence of civic piety also—as in the Warner case—identifies a host of other kinds of symbolic life within the society. Thus, under such an approach, it becomes increasingly difficult to establish the distinction between the evidence for the hypothesized religious institution of the culture and other phenomena. By that same measure, the kind of evidence alleged as proof for the reality of civil religion can also be assimilated to other frameworks perceived to be necessary to interpret the other symbolic phenomena.

Concepts of public religion that identify cultural values as a religious framework draw on different although related traditions of analysis. Religion is interpreted less as the symbolic and ritual expression of actual social unity (in the terms suggested by Durkheim) that it is comprehended as functioning to maintain a coherent society. What receives attention in these models is not so much explicit rituals or beliefs as the sentiments which render a society one because all members share a value set. A widely quoted statement of this position was offered by Robin Williams in his sociological analysis of modern America.[18] The position is generally accepted and frequently reiterated in sociological literature.

> Every functioning society has to an important degree a *common* religion. The possession of a common set of ideas, rituals, and symbols can supply an overarching sense of unity even in a society riddled with realistic conflicts. . . .[19]

This statement and others like it which take essentially the same position do derive from Durkheim in important respects. At the same time, emphasis is shifted (1) to the functioning of value orientations as they operate at an instrumental level to support social solidarity, and (2) away from the collectivity as object of the religion. Analysis of public religion in this framework results in judicious attention to the empirical varieties and unities of manifest religious life and the characteristics of the social matrix represented through them. This perspective on religious phenomena in American society thus tends to reduce piety to (in the sense of interpret in terms of) those values which motivate and guide behavior within this as well as any society.

The fullest utilization of this type of model of public religion is to be found in Will Herberg's *Protestant-Catholic-Jew*.[20] The central theme of this book is the development of three subcultures in American society based on the religious traditions identified in the title. But a subordinate and closely related theme is that these traditions had become, in effect, versions of one American culture. Each is interpreted as a variant expression, albeit under different sets of symbols, of a common culture—the American Way of Life.[21] Herberg essentially interprets the

American Way of Life as the operative common religion of American society. It embodies that set of values basic to the American social order. Indeed, Herberg identifies this "spiritual structure" as a civic religion, and with some warrant, it can be claimed that the formal discussion of civil religion in America begins here.[22]

In Herberg's elaboration of this insight, he looked primarily for common values as the substance of the American culture, although he also gave some attention to the beliefs and rituals which were associated with them. He analyzed the particular set of values he believed to lie at the heart of American society as a kind of secularized puritanism, adopting a particular list which had been suggested by Dorothy Canfield Fisher in her discussion of *The Vermont Character.*[23] By extension, this type of analysis can appropriate a great deal from the considerable literature which has undertaken to identify the American character. There are substantial resources in studies of that genre to delineate the common values of the society as they have been preserved and transformed through time. Extension of the present discussion in that direction would lead away, however, from the central purpose of this chapter, which is to indicate ideal-typical models in terms of which piety in the public realm has been conceptualized and discussed.

This cultural-value model for public religion entails less theoretical baggage than constructs of the first type, which, while developing out of much the same tradition of sociological thought, emphasize that society itself is the object of religious behavior and the reference for religious symbols in given social orders. This second model, by contrast, emphasizes the functions of such symbols—that is, the mechanisms through which they contribute to the maintenance of the social order.

A third type of model or concept shifts emphasis to

differentiated political society and the role of religious behaviors and beliefs within it. The term civil religion was proposed by Rousseau, who is an intellectual grandfather of the traditions of thought which conceive society as sacred or cultural values as the embodiment of public religion.[24] In Rousseau's discussion, however, the problematic to be addressed was the civil ordering of society or its government. Of course, this was an ancient agenda made all the more pressing in the eighteenth century by the application of premises current in the Enlightenment to the understanding of the political fabric in general and the government as a differentiated institution of society in particular.

In turning to Rousseau's discussion, it is clear that this different set of assumptions operates. Rousseau is not concerned with symbols and functions, but with rights, duties, and obligations. This is the classical language of political thought. Rousseau explicitly reserves to citizens the right to private opinions.[25] What does concern a sovereign, in his view, is that opinions and beliefs have implications for the political community. It is only with reference to morality and duties to others that dogmas of religion concern the state.[26] The state may enter the realm of religious concerns to prescribe appropriate beliefs because of the operational or instrumental relationship of religion to the community. (This relationship is not conceived in terms of functions or values, but in terms of political behavior as derived from belief.) Thus, Rousseau would have the sovereign "fix the articles" of a "purely civil profession of faith." These are not, apparently, thought to be exactly "religious dogmas, but . . . social sentiments without which a man cannot be a good citizen or a faithful subject."[27] When the inquiry is pressed what these dogmas might be, Rousseau's response is reminiscent of the answers given in the tradition of deistic thought: belief in God, providence, immortality, commitment to the justness of life, the "sanctity of the social contract and the laws," and tolerance for other beliefs.[28] These articles of a civic creed, Rousseau believed, would be conducive to political stability.

This concept of civic piety subsumes a very ancient heritage. At the very least it may be traced back to the imperial roman program of agreeing to tolerate tolerating religions, with the critical test or proof being expression of allegiance to the imperial cult.[29] Like Rousseau's civil religion, the cult was developed in the framework of the necessity of political order and was directed to the achievement of ends within the political realm. Of course emphasis on civic piety does not preclude understanding society as sacred or cultural values as the means to a deeper social cohesion. But this model directs attention to political behavior and belief as the social location in which civic piety will be manifest.

In the American case there certainly are grounds for construing conventional understandings of patriotism in the terms of this construct. A classical expression was the initial flag salute case—Minersville School District, *et al. v. Gobitis et al.*—decided by the Supreme Court in 1940.[30] (The case was concluded prior to United States entry into World War II, and well before confidence engendered by anticipated victory for the Allied cause permitted the civil libertarian position to have a greater claim on the public conscience.) The Pennsylvania school board had moved to require a flag salute from every school child as an explicit sign of patriotic allegiance to the United States of America. Acting on the basis of the claims made on their consciences by their convictions as Jehovah's Witnesses, the Gobitis children refused. In the setting of the pre-war years, they were prosecuted, and the case finally made its way to the Supreme Court in 1940. The language used by the Court in sustaining the requirement that the children be held accountable for refusing to salute the flag classically represents the argument for civic piety as a requirement placed upon citizens in order to assure political stability. This political loyalty is not thought to entail abridgement of opinions which do not touch upon belief and behavior in the political context. In deciding to sustain the Pennsylvania practice on the basis of a philosophy of judicial restraint, it clearly delineated a framework rooted in classical political theory of which Rousseau's reflections on civil religion were a part:

A society which is dedicated to the preservation of . . . ultimate values of civilization may in self-protection utilize the educational process for inculcating those almost unconscious feelings which bind men together in a comprehending loyalty, whatever may be their lesser differences and difficulties. That is to say, the process may be utilized so long as men's right to believe as they please, to win others to their way of belief, and their right to assemble in their chosen places of worship for the devotional ceremonies of their faith, are fully respected.[31] (The opinion was written by Justice Frankfurter.)

Viewed in the context of the development and refinement of American civil liberties, the important point is that the Court returned to consider the issue of compulsory flag salute in public schools three years later. West Virginia State Board of Education *et al. v.* Barnette *et al.* (1943) is a noteworthy case because the Supreme Court explicitly acknowledged that its previous position in the Gobitis case was in error, a most unusual event in the life of that august court of last resort within the American system. The Barnette case is a landmark case on other grounds too, however, because it represents the first instance in the history of the Court in which substantial civil rights are held to be guaranteed under the religion clauses of the First Amendment. Barnette was extremely important in beginning the process of delineating the precise positive grant or content of these important clauses of the Bill of Rights.[32]

In the context of a discussion of models of public religion in America, of course, these cases are a rather different exhibit. Gobitis presents in lucid form a modern version of the argument for civic piety by emphasizing the central importance of common religious beliefs and behaviors (construed in relatively positivistic ways) to political society, and by identifying that common religion as explicitly linked to a nation-state. In this framework, Barnette represents a significant critique of an exclusive and narrow construction of civic piety under American law.

In this third model, the mode of religious representation has shifted to a particular political regime. Thus, civic piety is a well-differentiated set of beliefs and behaviors that signifies loyalty to a sharply defined political structure— indeed, in the extreme case, to a particular regime at a particular time. Such civic piety is not necessarily in tension with cultural values or even with the sacralization of a particular society. But as a theoretical framework of analysis, it is distinct and does not require either of the others as a model in terms of which public religion might be studied.

A fourth and final model represents a significantly

different construct. Here the mode of religious representation entails the projection of a framework of meaning into a transcendental realm. In the American case this means adopting a framework of interpretation for the collective life which identifies a particular origin and a special destiny for the nation. It becomes, in the mythic framework, the vehicle for purposes attributed to the cosmos. The best example of this type of concept is to be found in the writings of Sidney Mead.[33] In various addresses and essays, Mead has advocated the uniqueness of what he has termed "The Religion of the Republic." This is an interpretation of the sources, mission, and destiny of the American Republic which he traces to the Enlightenment, although, in a yet larger perspective, it is viewed as fulfillment of Western Christian history.[34] For Mead, the Enlightenment was above all a religious turning point in human history, for, understood properly, it represented the liberation of Western humanity from subjection to the tyrannical hold of superstition and from the shackles of political domination. In the positive construction Mead gives it, the Enlightenment meant that humankind could now take its fate into its own hands, hearts, and minds, so to speak, and achieve progress toward genuine liberation through the means of republican political communities. This possibility, Mead believes, was uniquely available, or available to a unique degree, to Americans; and the foundation of the United States as a new nation was this commitment to the civil and religious development of humanity. Thus for Mead, the public religion of America is the explicit affirmation of this destiny through a "Religion of the Republic."

Mead's particular views should be consulted in greater detail and with care since they represent a more strictly theological construction of public religion and one more manifestly American than the other types already noted. Mead's Religion of the Republic is less a separate body of theory or school of social thought than commitment to a theological modality which works upon historical materials with little interest in the analysis of religion as a differentiated aspect of social life in modern settings. Finally, it is deeply dependent upon the enlightenment-rationalist-Unitarian tradition of religion in American culture. But it is the logical end point of the continuum of models for public religion, which runs from a society as its own sacred object through progressively greater differentiation of religion to a society as subject of sacred intentions.

The continuum we have proposed is a logical construct which will have served its chief purpose if it establishes the interdependence of evidence and interpretation in the analysis of piety in the public realm. It may also help to explain both the source of the widespread confusion in the general discussion of this topic and the ambiguity already noted in Robert Bellah's proposal that there is a civil religion in America. In particular, the latter discussion synthesized elements from most of the models of the continuum suggested above. This gave a richness of texture to the civil religion proposal in terms of the phenomena cited. But what was not included, as far as I can determine, was reflection upon the broader issue: What would an "elaborate and well institutionalized" civil religion "alongside of and rather clearly differentiated from the Churches" really look like? It is often true that making explicit a framework of analysis for, as an example, a play or a poem may work to trivialize it. No less than in literary criticism, religious and social criticism runs the risk of contributing to such a result. But failure to refine poor criticism into more sophisticated criticism amounts to irresponsibility in the life of the intellect. More explicit attention to this issue is required in the civil religion discussion.

Some serious attemps at modelling what *a discrete religion* looks like are readily available. Such models provide frameworks for analysis of particular religions and make possible comparisons between them. Among the more useful, because rather internally complex and responsive to the range of phenomena involved, is that offered by Anthony F. C. Wallace, who works from an anthropological perspective upon culture.[35] In his model, he directs attention to certain "universal formal properties" which amount to "the skeletal anatomy" of religion, although there is variety and even significant modification from species to species within the genus. His fundamental pattern discriminates certain levels of analysis. One level is "the supernatural premise." A second is certain "universal categories of religious behaviour," which Wallace identifies as "elementary particles of ritual," such as prayer, exhortation, sacrifice, symbolism. At a third level these elements are combined into "sequences called ritual." In turn, ritual is rationalized as belief. A final analytic level represents the organization of these rituals and beliefs into complexes recognized as "cult institutions," or "conglomerates," in which components from the preceding levels are integrated.

This kind of model is impressive and useful because it is predicated upon a rich field of discrete elements without the presence of which there is no proper subject. But it also requires that these elements become evidence for a particular religion only insofar as they interact in terms approximating the various levels of the model. The joining of elementary particles, for example, without the supernatural premise does not create *religious* ritual. Therefore, it is not enough to identify particular ritual phenomena as evidence for a religion; they become evidence for the latter only as they prove to be convincingly interpreted or set in terms of a framework which fulfills the basic conditions of the model. On this view, no particular act or belief is inherently religious (or irreligious), but each instance takes on that property only insofar as it is effectively interpreted as part of an overall formal pattern which approximates the above model.

An approach to understanding a particular religion which emphasizes basic elements organized in terms of fields feels right to residents of religiously plural societies. In such settings the same discrete act or particular belief, taken in abstraction, may be religiously indifferent for a Roman Catholic Christian while highly charged for an Orthodox Jew. Thus it is that religions have such deep holds on their adherents; religions work to organize experience of the world and actions within it, attaching both negative and positive values to various specific behaviors and beliefs. Anthony Wallace's exposition of a model for religion is particularly relevant to serious discussion of civil religion. But it is not necessary to accept his as the only possible or the finally correct model of religion in terms of which public religion must be interpreted. Other kinds of approaches to critical models of religion—some more philosophical, other more historical—might be adopted. The important point is that some such construct must illuminate the discussion of civil religion if it is to be seriously proposed that there is a developed and differentiated public religious construct in American culture.

The implication of the foregoing analysis is that a civil religion conforming to the requisite criteria has not been a continuing part of our national history, although it is not in doubt that pieties and religious episodes have been frequent and prominent. This conclusion does not imply that the civil religion discussion should be dismissed as unimportant. On the contrary, it has helped to render more subtle and nuanced the analysis of religion in a modern society readily accessible for close order analysis. If the case for a developed and differentiated civil religion in American history is at best questionable, that also does not foreclose the possibility that such a cult is now emerging or will in the future. Such a development remains hypothetical at this point. But what is established as a given is that the existence of American civil religion has been *proposed* at a particular point in the national experience. What religious interpretation should be placed upon that development will concern us in a brief concluding epilogue.

Epilogue

THE CIVIL RELIGION PROPOSAL AS A REVITALIZATION MOVEMENT IN AMERICAN CULTURE

The preceding chapters have explored public religion in America in terms of the relationship between the society and its national polity on the one hand, and piety (or ritual practices and attendant beliefs) on the other. The procedure has entailed exploration of various aspects of the question, ranging from a survey of relevant phenomena (construed in looser as well as tighter frameworks of analysis) to review of the kinds of models in terms of which data might be interpreted. In conclusion, we return to an issue which emerged at the outset—namely, that within the last decade discussion of public religion has entered a new stage in the proposal that it be understood as a differentiated and institutionalized positive religious tradition, as in "Civil Religion in America." That thesis has already been reviewed as a construction put upon the data, but brief consideration of it from another point of view is appropriate. This is to ask several questions in the framework of religious analysis: How may we interpret the development of the proposal that there is a civil religion in America? What significance should we assign to the emergence of a religious movement based upon such a proposal?

Elaboration of religiously grounded claims frequently entails an explicit historical trajectory set out in terms of

169

origin and destiny. Under Robert Bellah's construct, the American civil religion is believed to point toward a world order; its destiny is to become transformed into a global civil religion. The religion of the republic, the construction proposed by Sidney Mead, is thought to carry the burden of a cultural revolution originating with the Enlightenment. This event, possibly the most momentous cultural event in history, is believed to reach fullest expression in the ideal of the American republic.[1] Thus, each of these particular constructs includes a historical interpretation placed upon public religion cast in terms of universalistic claims. When viewed with some detachment, however, both of these proposals appear to be highly ethnocentric. In the framework of a critical approach to religious movements, the logically necessary question is how such worldviews function as social constructions. How might we understand the appeal of civil religion, or the religion of the republic, as the basis for a social movement?

One of the conditions under which religious movements appear to develop is that of rapid social change, especially when an older and possibly waning culture is threatened by a newer and dynamic one. Anthropologists have identified numerous instances of this kind of phenomenon. The cargo-cults of New Guinea have become a classical example on the basis of the excellent field reports and associated analysis which we have about them. The cults are usefully understood as millenarian movements, as responses in the idioms at hand—so to speak—to perceived threats from superior cultures.[2] Movements for revival or renewal of North American Indian cultures developed under broadly comparable conditions. Anthony F. C. Wallace has suggested an analytical model of the revitalization movement as a means of conceptualizing how a beleaguered society reaches for religious self-understanding out of the past, in terms which are familiar from the tradition at hand. This is a means of coping with an uncertain present and a threatening future.[3] In this most general framework, revitalization movements are interpreted as attempts to recover, heighten, and strenuously advocate adherence to the religious legacy believed to be the center of the particular endangered culture. The anticipated outcome is preservation of that culture, possibly including the achievement of a more perfect embodiment of its central commitments. Of course, in a critical perspective, the recovered or revitalized culture is actually different from the older one. It has undergone a selective adaptation. In that process, elements have been damped or heightened and the whole reorganized, usually in response to particular interest groups in the society.

If we seek an interpretation of the recent proposals about public religion in America in terms available from critical studies of religious movements, we can probably do no better than to view them as potential revitalization movements occasioned by widespread loss of internal confidence in American society and changed external cultural relationships.[4] It is obvious that sub-cultures, such as those of black Americans or Spanish-speaking Americans (and a host of others), have become ethnically self-conscious enough to call into question the viability of traditional American society. This is in part because a broadly Protestant hegemony is experienced as alien and oppressive. Those sensitive to this situation have responded in different ways. One kind of response to this perceived condition has been resonance to the call for recovery of a civil religion or religion of the republic. While the manifest symbols of these proposals may be universal and global, the latent basis for interest in and support of them has more likely been a concern that the old familiar ways are directly challenged and severely threatened.

Interestingly enough, from this perspective, the ideological contents of revitalization movements turn out to be culturally specific versions of American Protestant Christianity, more classical than modern, which have been given a content of broadly political symbols and events. These constructs, in line with accepted critical interpretations of such movements, probably have more currency as reconceptualizations of past ideologies than as direct continuations of them.

Why should an idealized past be so prominent in these proposals? Partly because particular versions of Protestantism have repeatedly proved to be divisive, especially in the American setting. But at least as important, the latent strategy of a revitalization movement is to counter a threat to the whole social fabric and, generally, to enlist Americans under more inclusive symbols and commitments than the narrower inherited construction would permit. In some respects, then, it may be helpful to interpret the civil religion phenomenon more properly as a latent political revitalization movement than as a manifestly religious one. At one level, this is because politics is the realm in which consensus is achieved in modern societies in spite of other divergent opinions. But at another level, the perceived threat may be that politics as a means of governing communities is proving to be anachronistic; societies seem less readily subject to control through classical political means. If this is the felt threat, the culture threatened is one in which the political process is taken seriously as a means of significantly affecting society.

On this view, it could be argued that we are passing beyond an era in which politics was the accepted means to resolve social conflict. This era began in the seventeenth century after the prolonged religious struggles in Europe seemed to demonstrate that institutions and practices based upon religious frameworks of intelligibility could not cope with the deep changes wracking the social orders. The wars of religion, on this view, marked the end of an epoch in European history. Religious language proved unable to produce intelligibility in the social world, and religious ritual failed to bring tolerable coherence to society. The arena of political life in the modern world, one of compromise, manipulation, agreement, and, as a last resort only, force, developed to confront these issues directly. On this hypothetical scenario, the era of the world wars in the twentieth century might appear, in retrospect, to have been the period in which classical political skills proved to be outmoded as means of contending with social change. In the place of this outmoded world—of both intelligibility and action—a new one will undoubtedly emerge, likely predicated upon economic management. This would seem to be the effective means currently available to control societies which cannot be ordered through political action, in the way that the European lands of the seventeenth century could not be governed within essentially religious frameworks of belief and behavior.

This kind of perspective is interesting because the manifest ends directly sought through movements like an American civil religion—especially universal political communities—appear more likely to be achieved indirectly. Ironically, the maligned multi-national corporation may prove to be a more effective vehicle for achieving a stable world order than either ecumenical activities among the traditional religious communities or a vital United Nations (even one supported through global civil religious commitments). A broadly economic framework which seeks to relate perceived self-interests to awareness of interdependence probably has promise of being more effective than explicitly universal religious or political world views.

As a large framework, this is a suggestion that the civil religion proposal be viewed as a political-religious revitalization movement at a transition point to new global arrangements based on more strictly economic calculations. This may seem to be an interpretive framework which is implicitly based on a model in which a secularization of modern cultures is the central given. That is not necessarily the case. Such large-scale frameworks do entail many other issues than the ones strictly at issue in this discussion of public religion. It does seem possible to suspend judgment about whether such a hypothetical process as we have suggested must entail a full-scale secularization framework. Instead, we might direct attention to more modest and more empirical observations, such as have formed the basic material of the study.

If by suggesting that the American civil religion proposal may be identified as the ideological core of a revitalization movement, we have seemed to diminish its significance (by associating it with the Ghost Dance movement, as an example), that is unfortunate. Better parallels to it might be found in such religio-social movements as pietism in the German Lands (and others) in the eighteenth century, or Stuart Puritanism in seventeenth-century England. Versions of millenarianism in nineteenth-century America may provide a yet closer parallel, even antecedent. The point is that in each case an older culture was deeply challenged by new social conditions, and its existence seemed to be threatened. As a cultural strategy, it moved to consolidate and reexpress what it took to be its essential commitments. Usually through a prophet or a cadre of leaders, the movement worked to conserve the old in the face of social change. So the civil religion proposal, or the advocacy of a religion of the republic, might be seen, finally, as the attempt, through a variety of particular forms, to distill the old political culture of the United States

which was supported by a broadly Protestant establishment. The purpose is to conserve that culture even as it,
and the associated establishment, is threatened from
within and without. Should the political culture prove to
be resilient and thus durable, it is likely that the American
civil religion proposal will either be forgotten as a curious
cultural episode, or celebrated as central to a renewed
nationalism. Should the alternative scenario develop, and
the political culture be finally displaced by a broadly
economic culture, then we might expect it to remain as a
fossilized ingredient in our society, though increasingly
peripheral to central concerns of the latter and with
progressively less influence upon it. In either case, the
current study has argued that the civil religion proposal
marks a particular construction of the public religion issue
in American history and it must be set in that framework
rather than interpreted in its own terms.

In a study of this sort, marked by the attempt to search
beneath appearances to more fundamental if elusive
reality, ironic detachment may seem to be the one
constant. Accordingly, the concluding observation is
properly ironic. Robert Bellah suggested that "Civil Religion in America" had gone undetected precisely because a
western concept of religion as differentiated had pre-
vented observers from recognizing something so obvious.
Americans resist acknowledging in their own culture, he
thought, something as obvious as Shinto in a foreign
culture.[5] But the further irony may be that emphasis upon
civil religion itself betrays the other side of that same
impulse—namely, to conceive of religion as developed and
institutionalized. The materials reviewed in the course of
this study seem not to require that interpretation, but are
better understood as aspects of an incredibly rich and
internally complex culture.

Notes

Chapter 1

1. Published in *The Writings of James Madison,* ed. G. Hunt, Volume IX (1819–1836) (N.Y., 1910), pp. 484–88.

2. *Ibid.*

3. *Ibid.*

4. Published in *The Writings of Thomas Jefferson,* ed. H. A. Washington, Volume VIII (N.Y., 1854), pp. 113–14.

5. Readily available in *Benjamin Franklin: Representative Selections,* ed. F. L. Mott and C. E. Jorgenson (N.Y., 1936), pp. 199–206.

6. *Ibid.,* p. 203.

7. For discussion of this question, see Daniel J. Boorstin, *The Lost World of Thomas Jefferson* (Boston, 1960), especially Chapter 3, section 2, pp. 119–27.

8. For an eloquent statement of this position, see W. E. Channing, "Spiritual Freedom," in *The Works of William E. Channing* (Boston, 1878), pp. 172–86.

9. (Chicago, 1968).

10. (N.Y., 1970).

11. (N.Y., 1971).

12. The monographic literature is extensive. An accessible and useful bibliographical list may be found in Sydney Ahlstrom, *A Religious History of the American People* (New Haven, 1972).

13. See Joseph Story, *Commentaries on the Constitution of the United States,* Volume III (Boston, 1833), especially pp. 722ff.

14. See Francis J. Grund, *The Americans* (Boston, 1837), pp. 163–64.

15. *Ibid.,* p. 165.

16. *Ibid.,* p. 166.

17. See *Democracy in America,* trans. H. Reeve, Volume I (N.Y., 1955), pp. 310ff.

18. *Ibid.,* p. 316.

19. James Dixon, *Personal Narrative* (N.Y., 1849), p. 191.

20. *Ibid.,* pp. 191–92.

21. Sidney Mead has popularized the phrase through an essay so titled which originally appeared in *Church History,* XXXVI (September 1967), pp. 262–83.

22. Especially relevant materials on Lincoln include William J. Wolf, *The Almost Chosen People* (Garden City,

L.I., 1959), and Edmund Wilson, "Abraham Lincoln: The Union as Religious Mysticism," in *Eight Essays* (Garden City, L.I., 1954).

23. David M. Potter suggests this interpretation. See his essay, "The Historian's Use of Nationalism and Vice Versa," in *History and American Society*, ed. D. E. Fehrenbacher (N.Y., 1973).

24. Schaff's essay was titled "Church and State in the United States" and published in *Papers of the American Historical Association*, Volume II, number 4 (N.Y., 1888). Quotation from p. 16.

25. Bryce's discussion was part of *The American Commonwealth* (N.Y., 1893). Quotation from revised edition (N.Y., 1914), Vol. II, p. 770.

26. General discussion of these developments may be followed in Ahlstrom, *A Religious History of the American People*.

27. *Protestant-Catholic-Jew* (Garden City, L.I., 1955).

28. Subsequent related discussions included A. Roy Eckardt, *The Surge of Piety in America* (N.Y., 1958), and Martin E. Marty, *The New Shape of American Religion* (N.Y., 1959).

29. See especially Chapter 11, "Religion in America in the Perspective of Faith."

30. Herberg's book at the same time embodied both descriptive and critical sides, and on the latter question numerous commentators joined his lament about the reality he had identified. *Ibid.*

31. The grand theme underlying Ahlstrom's magisterial volume is that the religious history of America was dominated by a Puritan culture originating under the Protestant monarch Elizabeth I (1560). Its decisive importance is drastically reduced by the second half of the twentieth century, during which (in 1960) the first Roman Catholic layman becomes President of the American republic.

32. "Civil Religion in America," in *Daedalus*, Volume 96, number 1, pp. 1–21.

Chapter 2

1. (Garden City, L.I., 1966).

2. See *The Invisible Religion* (N.Y., 1967).

3. See *The Sacred Canopy* (Garden City, L.I., 1967), especially Appendix I, "Sociological Definitions of Religion."

4. *Ibid.*, p. 33.

5. First published in *Anthropological Approaches to the Study of Religion* (N.Y., 1966), ed. Michael Banton, pp. 1–46. Republished in *The Interpretation of Cultures* (N.Y., 1973).

6. *The Interpretation of Cultures,* p. 90.

7. A theme central to Robert Bellah, *Civil Religion in America.*

8. This theme has been associated with Erich Auerbach's discussion of the characteristics of the literary tradition stemming from ancient Israel. See Hans Frei, *The Eclipse of Biblical Narrative* (New Haven, 1974).

9. This was a preoccupation in the writings of many Protestant thinkers involved with neo-orthodoxy. See, for example, Reinhold Niebuhr, *The Nature and Destiny of Man* (N.Y., 1943) and *Faith and History* (N.Y., 1949).

10. Perhaps the best approach to this question is through *God's New Israel* ed. Conrad Cherry (Englewood Cliffs, N.J., 1971).

11. See H. R. Niebuhr, *The Kingdom of God in America* (N.Y., 1935).

12. See James F. Maclear, "New England and the Fifth Monarchy: The Quest for the Millennium in Early American Puritanism," *Wil-*

liam and Mary Quarterly, Series 3, Volume 32 (1975), pp. 223–60.

13. A position broadly represented in the post-millennialism of nineteenth-century America. See E. L. Tuveson, *Redeemer Nation* (Chicago, 1968).

14. This distinction (actually he opposed Ethical to Exemplary) was utilized by Max Weber as a means of distinguishing between different kinds of prophets. It may also serve the purpose of distinguishing between different constructions of national collective self-understanding. See *Sociology of Religion,* trans. E. Fischoff (Boston, 1963).

15. The address is readily accessible in *The Puritans,* Volume I, ed. P. G. Miller (N.Y., 1963), pp. 195–99.

16. This theme was developed by Perry Miller in "Errand into the Wilderness," which gives the title to a collection of his essays (Cambridge, Mass., 1956).

17. A typical liberal reconstruction in the mid-twentieth century, especially in the context of struggles against fascism and communism.

18. See the extensive passages re. relations with other

nations. The Farewell Address may be consulted in *The Writings of George Washington,* ed. James C. Fitzpatrich, Volume 35 (Washington, 1940); see especially pp. 231–36.

19. It is crucial to emphasize that this element of American self-understanding is rooted in the same colonial beginnings.

20. *Democracy in America,* trans. Henry Reeve, 2 Volumes (N.Y., 1955).

21. Most fully studied by Bernard Bailyn in *The Ideological Origins of the American Revolution* (Cambridge, Mass., 1967).

22. A position argued most forcefully by Alan Heimert in *Religion and the American Mind* (Cambridge, Mass., 1966).

23. See the discussion by Seymour M. Lipset, *The First New Nation* (N.Y., 1967).

24. Conrad Cherry's edited volume illustrates the significance of the image throughout American history *(God's New Israel).* See also Catharine Albanese, *Sons of the Fathers* (Philadelphia, 1976) for a broader discussion of symbolism in the revolutionary era.

25. See the recent study by Nathan Hatch, *The Sacred Cause of Liberty* (New Haven, 1977).

26. A theme persuasively developed by William Haller in *The Rise of Puritanism* (N.Y., 1938).

27. See William Haller, *The Elect Nation* (N.Y., 1963) for a discussion of John Foxe's importance for English culture of the seventeenth century.

28. Classical elements were already present in colonial New England culture. They became even more pronounced in the periods of the War for Independence and the early republic. See Richard M. Gummere, *The American Colonial Mind and the Classical Tradition* (Cambridge, Mass., 1963), and Gordon S. Wood, *The Creation of the American Republic, 1776–1787* (Chapel Hill, 1969), Ch. II, sect. 2.

29. A theme developed by Joachim Wach, *Sociology of Religion* (Chicago, 1944), pp. 341–44.

30. On Luther, see Eric Erikson, *Young Man Luther* (N.Y., 1958). On Wesley, see G. Elsie Harrison, *Son to Sussanah* (Nashville, 1938).

31. This is a theoretical point only in the context of the present discussion.

32. A point emphasized by Catharine Albanese in *Sons of the Fathers,* pp. 143ff.

33. *Ibid.;* see also Wesley

Frank Craven, *The Legend of the Founding Fathers* (N.Y., 1956).

34. See John W. Ward, *Andrew Jackson: Symbol for an Age* (N.Y., 1962).

35. See two interesting discussions of Lincoln and religion: Edmund Wilson, "Abraham Lincoln: The Union as Religious Mysticism," in *Eight Essays* (Garden City, L.I., 1954), and William J. Wolf, *The Almost Chosen People* (Garden City, L.I., 1959).

36. The procedure through which saints are canonized within the Roman Catholic tradition provides at least an institutionalized analogy to, if not a rationalized version of, this more general process within human collectivities.

37. Gordon Wood's study, *The Creation of the American Republic,* is the most comprehensive analysis.

38. David M. Potter has dealt with the relationship between the Civil War and American nationalism; see "The Historian's Use of Nationalism and Vice Versa," readily available in *History and American Society,* ed. D. E. Fehrenbacher (N.Y., 1973).

39. For a discussion of the covenant tradition in New England culture, see Robert G. Pope, *The Half-Way Cove-*

nant (Princeton, 1969).

40. A recent sustained discussion in Cushing Strout, *The New Heavens and New Earth* (N.Y., 1974).

Chapter 3

1. See *Public Papers of the President Dwight D. Eisenhower 1953* (Washington, 1960), p. 1.

2. See Will Herberg's discussion of this comment in *Protestant-Catholic-Jew* (Garden City, L.I., 1960), p. 84.

3. See, especially, Emile Durkheim, *The Elementary Forms of Religious Life,* trans. Joseph W. Swain (N.Y., 1965).

4. Louis Hartz has explored relevant aspects of American society, especially the absence of traditional elements typical of Europe, in *The Liberal Tradition in America* (N.Y., 1955). He has also suggested the larger framework of European colonization of the new world within which the American case fits; see *The Founding of New Societies* (N.Y., 1964).

5. These assertions are staple observations in the analysis of religion in American history.

6. "Civil Religion in

America," *Daedalus,* Volume 96, number 1, p. 5.

7. See "American Civil Religion in the 1970s," in *American Civil Religion,* ed. Russell Richey and Donald Jones (N.Y., 1974), pp. 255–72.

8. In attempting to gauge the presidential materials with respect to this question, I have made use of various collections of documents, since the practice of issuing formal editions of presidential state papers was begun recently and critical and complete collected editions of the papers of presidents is underway with respect to the more important only. *The Inaugural Addresses . . . From 1789 . . . to . . . 1969* is available as House Document 91–142 (Washington, D.C., 1969). Washington's First Inaugural is on pp. 1–4, references are *passim.*

9. *Ibid.,* pp. 7–45, *passim.*

10. *Ibid.,* pp. 47 and 53.

11. *Ibid.,* pp. 55–117, *passim.*

12. *Ibid.,* pp. 125–26.

13. *Ibid.,* pp. 127–28.

14. *Ibid.,* pp. 169, 177, 180.

15. *Ibid.,* pp. 207, 213, 214.

16. *Ibid.,* pp. 215–43.

17. The quotation concludes the Third Inaugural (1941), *ibid.,* p. 247. See both addresses for the shift in tone, *ibid.,* pp. 244–49.

18. *Ibid.,* pp. 267–70.

19. *Ibid.,* p. 256 (see also pp. 251–56).

20. *Ibid.,* p. 257 (see also pp. 257–62).

21. *Ibid.,* pp. 263–66.

22. Thus the attempt to establish a "beachhead of cooperation" is to "push back the jungle of suspicion." *Ibid.,* p. 269.

23. The concluding peroration, "God's work must truly be our own," was addressed to "citizens of America" and "citizens of the world." *Ibid.,* pp. 270.

24. Seymour H. Fersh, *The View from the White House* (Washington, D.C., 1961).

25. *Ibid.,* p. 11.

26. *Ibid.,* p. 61.

27. *Ibid.*

28. *Ibid.,* pp. 76–77.

29. *Ibid.,* pp. 98–99.

30. *Ibid.,* p. 124.

31. *Ibid.,* pp. 124ff.

32. *Ibid.,* p. 125.

33. *A Compilation of Messages and Papers of the Presidents,* ed. James D. Richardson, 20 Volumes, (N.Y., 1897ff) has been cited (rather than the Washington edition, 10 Volumes, 1896–1898) because it is the more inclusive and was indexed to facilitate use. References are to Volume VIII, p. 3972.

34. *Ibid.,* Vol. IX, p. 4231.

35. This summary condensation is my own.

36. *Messages and Papers,* Vol. IX, p. 4231.

37. *Ibid.,* Vol. IX, pp. 4096, 4138.

38. See text of Nixon's proclamation as printed in the New York *Times,* November 18, 1972. (Officially published in the *Federal Register.*)

39. *Messages and Papers,* Vol. XI, pp. 5536–37.

40. *Ibid.,* Vol. XVI, pp. 8012–13; Vol. XVIII, pp. 9445–46.

41. The inference is drawn from the presidential materials.

42. *Messages and Papers,* Vol. I, p. 56.

43. Held on Thursday, February 19. *Ibid.,* Vol. I, pp. 171–72.

44. *Ibid.,* Vol. I, pp. 258–60.

45. *Ibid.,* Vol. I, pp. 274–76.

46. *Ibid.,* Vol. II, p. 498. See letter from Thomas Jefferson to the Reverend Mr. Millar, written January 23, 1808, in which he discusses his attitude toward the question of fast days. *The Writings of Thomas Jefferson,* ed. H. A. Washington, Volume V (Washington, D.C., 1853), pp. 236–38.

47. *Messages and Papers,* Vol. II, pp. 517–18, 543.

48. *Ibid.,* Vol. II, pp. 545–46.

49. *Ibid.,* materials concerning "humiliations" are located in Vol. VII, pp. 3237–38, 3365–66, 3422–23; materials concerning "thanksgivings" are located in Vol. VII, p. 3290, 3371, 3373–74, 3429–30.

50. *Ibid.,* Vol. XVI, p. 8007, Vol. XVI, pp. 8377–78.

51. *Ibid.,* Vol. XVII, pp. 8495–96.

52. *Ibid.,* Vol. IV, p. 1887.

53. *Ibid.,* Vol. VIII, p. 3504. The day was May 25.

54. *Ibid.,* Vol. VIII, p. 3505.

55. *Ibid.,* Vol. X, p. 4621.

56. *Ibid.,* Vol. XIII, p. 6639.

57. *Ibid.,* Vol. XVIII, pp. 9321–22.

58. See *Public Papers of the Presidents of the United States: Lyndon B. Johnson 1963–1964.* Book I (Washington, 1965), p. 2.

59. "The Kennedy Assassination and the Nature of Political Commitment" in *The Kennedy Assassination and the American Public,* ed. B. S. Greenberg and E. B. Parker (Stanford, 1965), pp. 359–60.

60. For a very human—and telling—report of how religious materials are developed for use by the president, see Frederic Fox, "The National Day of

Prayer," *Theology Today,* Volume XXIX, p. 3 (October, 1972), pp. 258–80.

Chapter 4

1. This generalization could be elaborated at great length and extensive evidence marshalled in its support.

2. See Laura Fermi, *Illustrious Immigrants: The Intellectual Migration from Europe, 1930–1941* (Chicago, 1968).

3. See, as one study by an anthropologist which tries to take American culture as a proper subject, Jules Henry, *Culture Against Man* (N.Y., 1963).

4. Sidney Verba, "The Kennedy Assassination and the Nature of Political Commitment," in *The Kennedy Assassination and the American Public,* ed. B. S. Greenberg and E. B. Parker (Stanford, 1965), pp. 359–60.

5. *Ibid.*

6. See his *Tokugawa Religion* (Glencoe, Ill., 1957), and *Religion and Progress in Modern Asia,* edited with an introduction and epilogue by Bellah (N.Y., 1965).

7. See *Democracy in America,* Volume I (N.Y., 1955), chapter XVII, especially sec-

tions regarding religion, pp. 310–26.

8. See, e.g., Volume II (N.Y., 1955), chapter V, pp. 21–29.

9. Michael Chevalier, *Society, Manners and Politics in the United States* (N.Y., 1969; first issued 1839).

10. *Ibid.,* p. 317.

11. *Ibid.*

12. *Ibid.,* p. 321.

13. This story apparently traces to Margaret Bayard Smith, *The First Forty Years of Washington Society,* ed. Gaillard Smith (N.Y., 1906), p. 12. Dumas Malone is skeptical of its authenticity. See *Jefferson the President: First Term 1801–1805,* Vol. 4, (Boston, 1970), p. 29.

14. See report in the New York *Times,* November 23, 1963. Judge S. T. Hughes administered the oath in the cabin of the presidential airplane. See p. 2.

15. Giscard d'Estaing has been characterized as a "French Kennedy," signifying an apparent attempt to introduce American patterns of political behavior into French culture. His campaign style and activities were discussed in an article in the New York *Times,* April 23, 1974, p. 6.

16. It is obvious that the

approach (and the outcomes) of Erving Goffman's work has intrigued me. See, for example, his *Interaction Ritual* (Garden City, L.I., 1967).

17. Conventional responses to the stridency of such tactics—amounting to disbelief that such behavior could characterize a manifestly liberal society—often made it difficult to perceive the nature of the symbiotic relationship: the protest premised the deeper pattern of behavior.

18. See Conrad Cherry, *God's New Israel*, (Englewood Cliffs, N.J., 1971), pp. 1–8. Also his essay, "American Sacred Ceremonies," in *American Mosaic*, ed. P. Hammond and B. Johnson (N.Y., 1970), pp. 303–16; and his essay, "Two American Sacred Ceremonies," in *American Quarterly*, Volume XXI, number 4 (1969), pp. 739–54.

19. Cherry, *God's New Israel*.

20. Of course the question raised by such phenomena is how they should be interpreted.

21. The decline in importance of Armistice Day (November 11) is surely linked to the passing of the generation which had fought World War I to "make the world safe for democracy." Memorial Day, by tradition involving military displays, became an obvious target for expression of antipathy to government war policies in the late 1960s. Its long-term fate in American culture remains an open question since in the very recent past there has been at least a partial return to earlier patterns of celebration.

22. This sketch could be amplified at great length with numerous illustrations.

23. See Bellah's original essay and Verba's reflections on the assassination of John F. Kennedy (see footnote 4 above).

24. (New Haven, 1959). *The Family of God* (New Haven, 1961), Part III, "The Living and the Dead," pp. 155–259, is the relevant section on Memorial Day in Yankee City, although without the sections which make the theoretical considerations explicit.

25. President Ford's ill-fated Whip Inflation Now campaign—WIN—is an obvious recent example of this point.

26. See works of Victor Turner, especially *The Ritual Process* (Chicago, 1969),

Dramas, Fields, and Metaphors (Ithaca, 1974), and *The Forest of Symbols* (Ithaca, 1967).

27. Mary Douglas, *Natural Symbols: Explorations in Cosmology* N.Y., 1970; second edition, London, 1973).

Chapter 5

1. For an essay which responds to the perceptions of plural meanings, see John Higham, "Hanging Together: Divergent Unities in American History," in *The Journal of American History,* Volume LXI (June 1974). With respect to the interpretation of American religious history, see my essay, "A Review of Some Reviews," in *Religious Studies Review* Volume I, number 1, pp. 1–8, which indicates how discussion of the question has developed around Sydney Ahlstrom's *A Religious History of the American People* (New Haven, 1972).

2. "Puritanism and Immigration," in *The Immigrant in American History* (Cambridge, 1940).

3. See my monograph, *Puritanism and the Public Realm* (Philadelphia, 1976), as an attempt to link this insight to other literatures.

4. Interest has recently developed in migration studies as a formal topic. See,

for example, various publications sponsored by Research Group for European Migration Problems.

5. The cultural implications in terms of the dominant white group are explored in Winthrop Jordan, *White Over Black* (Chapel Hill, 1968).

6. Seriously studied, for example, in St. Clair Drake and Horace R. Cayton, *Black Metropolis* (N.Y., 1945). For discussion of the religious aspects, see the summary chapter, "Negro Religion in the City," in E. F. Frazier, *The Negro Church in America* (N.Y., 1964).

7. Terms which have originated in analysis of possible political consequences of social change but which identify a phenomenon which has larger cultural implications as well.

8. The study *Protestant-Catholic-Jew,* by Will Herberg, was occasioned in important respects by the necessity to explore this development in American society after World War II.

9. A comparative study of puritanisms would be extremely valuable to complement the more conventional comparative studies of revolutions.

10. See *The Burned-Over*

District, by Whitney R. Cross (Ithaca, 1950).

11. See, as examples of this literature, Peter Worsely, *The Trumpet Shall Sound* (N.Y., 1968), Kenelm Burridge, *New Heaven, New Earth* (N.Y., 1969), Michael Barkun, *Disaster and the Millennium* (New Haven, 1974).

12. See, as examples of this literature, Norman Cohn, *The Pursuit of the Millennium* (N.Y., 1957), and *Millennial Dreams in a Nation,* ed. Sylvia Thrupp (N.Y., 1970).

13. This statement is not meant to be dependent upon a crude form of deprivation theory.

14. See, for example, the social psychological study of a modern cult, Leon Festinger, et al., *When Prophecy Fails* (Minneapolis, 1956).

15. See Louis Hartz, *The Liberal Tradition in America* (N.Y., 1955), for a study of American society as, in some sense, traditionless.

16. See Alan Heimert, *Religion and the American Mind* (Cambridge, 1966).

17. William A. Clebsch, *From Sacred to Profane America* (N.Y., 1968), proposes that central aspects of American society developed from sacred auspices to secular independence.

18. (N.Y., 1935).

19. There is a sense in which the development of the Kingdom symbol beyond the late nineteenth-century Social Gospel construction is to be traced into the Secular City discussion of the 1960s —and to the civil religion proposal.

20. (Chicago, 1968).

21. In one respect, episodes of cultural conflict, such as the rise of the counter-culture in the late 1960s, are generational struggles manifesting the importance of cultural meaning within the society.

22. See Laura Fermi, *Illustrious Immigrants: The Intellectual Migration From Europe, 1930–1941* (Chicago, 1968).

23. J. Hector St. John Crèvecoeur, *Letters from an American Farmer* (London, 1782). See the essay of that same title by A. M. Schlesinger, Sr., in *American Historical Review,* Volume XLVIII, and reprinted in *Paths to the Present* (N.Y., 1949).

24. From "The New Colossus" (1883).

25. Herberg's *Protestant-Catholic-Jew* should be seen as an attempt to update and refine the concept.

26. Oscar Handlin, *The Uprooted* (N.Y., 1951) is a classic portrayal of the

migration to America. For a
general discussion, see
Maldwyn A. Jones, *American
Immigration* (Chicago, 1960).

27. See Bernard Bailyn's
work for discussion of the
political culture, especially,
*The Ideological Origins of the
American Revolution* (Cambridge, 1967), and *The Origins
of American Politics* (N.Y.,
1969).

28. Taken to its extreme
in the religious commitment
to laissez-faire capitalism, as
in the Gospel of Wealth.

29. *Escape from Freedom*
(N.Y., 1941).

30. See David M. Potter,
People of Plenty (Chicago,
1954).

31. This strategy is similar
of that adopted by Sidney
Mead [in his article, "Denominationalism: The Shape
of Protestantism in America,"
in *Church History,* Volume
XXIII (December 1954), and
reprinted in *The Lively Experiment* (N.Y., 1963), pp.
103–33] and is similar to a
polythetic approach to classification used in anthropology.

Chapter 6

1. See his "Commentary"
on "Civil Religion in
America" in *The Religious
Situation: 1968,* ed. Donald R.
Cutler (Boston, 1968), pp.

381–88. See also a brief
discussion by Conrad Cherry
in "Two American Sacred
Ceremonies," *American
Quarterly,* Volume XXI,
number 4 (1969), pp. 750–
51.

2. Cutler, *Religious Situation,* p. 382.

3. *Ibid.*

4. *Ibid.,* pp. 382ff.

5. *Ibid.,* pp. 385ff.

6. Bellah's response to
"Commentary," in *ibid.,* p.
392.

7. *Ibid.,* p. 382.

8. A classic essay on this
question is H. R. Niebuhr,
The Social Sources of Denominationalism (N.Y., 1929).

9. See Edward Wakin and
Joseph Scheuer, *The De-Romanization of the American
Catholic Church* (N.Y., 1966).

10. See monograph by
Gibson Winter, *Religious
Identity* (N.Y., 1968). Also for
a more historical perspective,
see Mark deWolfe Howe, *The
Garden and the Wilderness*
(Chicago, 1965).

11. See John A. Hostetler,
Amish Society (Baltimore,
1963), and *Children in Amish
Society* (N.Y., 1971).

12. See George Kranzler,
Williamsburg, A Jewish Community in Transition (N.Y.,
1961), and Solomon Poll, *The
Hasidic Community of Williamsburg* (N.Y., 1962).

13. Such might be argued with respect to monasticism in the late Roman Empire. The subsequent history of religious communities suggests it may succeed as a strategy for a transitional period only.

14. See William A. Clebsch, *From Sacred to Profane America* (N.Y., 1968), for an extended essay on the role(s) of religion in American history. Chapter 4, "A Little Learning," discusses the question of education, pp. 104–38.

15. See an account and analysis of the episode in Cincinnati in Robert Michaelsen, *Piety in the Public Schools* (N.Y., 1970), pp. 89–106. On the parochial school issue, see David B. Tyack, "The Perils of Pluralism: The Background of the Pierce Case," in *American Historical Review*, Volume LXXIV (October 1968), pp. 74–98.

16. J. Paul Williams raised the substance of this issue some years ago in *The New Education and Religion* (N.Y., 1946), pp. 159–65.

17. See, as examples, Jonathan Kozol, *Death at an Early Age* (Boston, 1967), and *Free Schools* (Boston, 1972). Also see Ivan D. Illich, *Deschooling Society* (N.Y., 1971).

18. His most systematic statement was given as the Terry Lectures. John Dewey, *A Common Faith* (New Haven, 1952). See an account of Dewey's program in Michaelsen, *Piety*, pp. 140–49. Also see Horace M. Kallen, *Secularism is the Will of God*.

19. Williams' argument is developed in *What Americans Believe and How They Worship* (N.Y., 1952), chapter XIV, "The Role of Religion in Shaping American Destiny"; especially pp. 371ff.

20. Hammond, *Religious Situation*, p. 386

21. See Kai Erikson, *Wayward Puritans* (N.Y., 1966).

22. Originally published in *American Historical Review,* Volume L (1944–45), pp. 1–25. Republished without footnotes and with minor changes in *Paths to the Present* (N.Y., 1949), pp. 23–50.

23. See *Voluntary Associations,* ed. D.B. Robertson (Richmond, Va., 1966). Also see Constance Smith and Anne Freedman, *Voluntary Associations* (Cambridge, 1972).

24. See *Voluntary Action Research: 1974,* ed. D.H. Smith (Lexington, Ma., 1974).

25. The John Birch Society and Schwartz's Anti-Communist Crusade are well-known recent examples.

See an older study of such radical groups by Ralph Lord Roy, *Apostles of Discord* (Boston, 1953). A careful study of the phenomenon in nineteenth-century America is Wallace E. Davies, *Patriotism on Parade* (Cambridge, 1955).

26. Luther P. Gerlach and Virginia Hine, *People, Power, Change: Movements of Social Transformation* (Indianapolis, 1970), p. xvii.

Chapter 7

1. "Civil Religion in America," *Daedalus* (Winter 1967), pp. 1–21. This essay is widely available since it has been republished numerous times. It is easily accessible in: *Religion in America*, ed. Robert N. Bellah and William G. McLoughlin (Boston, 1968); *The Religious Situation: 1968*, ed. Donald R. Cutler (Boston, 1968); Robert N. Bellah, *Beyond Belief* (N.Y., 1970); and *American Civil Religion*, ed. Russell Richey and Donald Jones (N.Y., 1974). See also "Response" to comments on "Civil Religion in America" in Cutler, *The Religious Situation: 1968*; "American Civil Religion in the 1970s," in Richey and Jones, *American Civil Religion*;

Robert Bellah, *The Broken Covenant: American Civil Religion in Time of Trial* (N.Y., 1975); and "The Revolution and Civil Religion," in *Religion and the American Revolution*, ed. Jerald C. Brauer (Philadelphia, 1976).

2. A readily accessible collection of statements, with basic bibliography, is in Richey and Jones, *American Civil Religion*.

3. Bellah, "Civil Religion," p. 1.

4. *Ibid.*

5. *Ibid.*, p. 19.

6. In Emile Durkheim, *The Elementary Forms of Religious Life*, trans. J. W. Swain (N.Y., 1965).

7. Louis Hartz, *The Liberal Tradition in America*.

8. Seymour M. Lipset has interpreted American development as *The First New Nation* (Garden City, L.I., 1967)—that is, the first modern nation created by revolt against colonial regimes. David M. Potter's reflective essays on American society and culture approach some of these issues with great sensitivity; see his *People of Plenty*.

9. Bellah, "Civil Religion," p. 12.

10. Durkheim, *Elementary Forms*, p. 59.

11. *Ibid.*

12. *Ibid.*

13. *Ibid.*

14. This is made clear in the essay itself. See Bellah, "Civil Religion," fn. 1, p. 19. See also a reader in Durkheim edited by Bellah, *Emile Durkheim on Morality and Society* (Chicago, 1973).

15. W. Lloyd Warner, *The Living and the Dead* (New Haven, 1959).

16. The materials are part of an abridged version of *The Living and the Dead,* published as *The Family of God* (New Haven, 1961). The analysis of Memorial Day has been separately reprinted even without the richer setting provided by *The Family of God.* See W. Lloyd Warner, *American Life: Dream and Reality* (Chicago, 1953), and also "An American Sacred Ceremony," in Richey and Jones, *American Civil Religion.*

17. The theoretical sections of *The Living and the Dead,* which make plain the premises on the basis of which, and the framework within which, Warner analyzed the Memorial Day ceremonies, were not included in *The Family of God.* I think that it is unwarranted to use the analysis of that particular ceremony without giving serious attention to the theoretical framework that informs it.

18. Robin M. Williams, *American Society* (N.Y., 1951).

19. *Ibid.,* p. 312.

20. *Protestant-Catholic-Jew* (Garden City, L.I., 1955, 1960).

21. See chapter V, "The Religion of Americans and American Religion," in *ibid.,* pp. 72–98.

22. See Herberg's statement, "America's Civil Religion: What It Is and Whence It Comes," in Richey and Jones, *American Civil Religion,* pp. 76–88.

23. Herberg, *Protestant-Catholic-Jew,* pp. 80–81.

24. Rousseau's discussion is in *The Social Contract,* Book IV, chapter 8, "Civil Religion."

25. (London, 1913), p. 120.

26. *Ibid.,* p. 121.

27. *Ibid.*

28. *Ibid.*

29. A study of the imperial cult in the context of the religious pluralism of the Roman Empire, without the Christian bias which distorts many discussions of it, would contribute to development of comparative perspectives on American civil religion.

30. Important church-state cases were reprinted in a collection edited by Joseph

Tussman, *The Supreme Court on Church and State* (N.Y., 1962). Gobitis is on pp. 80–90.

31. *Ibid.*, pp. 85ff.

32. *Ibid.*, pp. 142–70.

33. See especially the essay, "The 'Nation with the Soul of a church,'" originally published in *Church History*, Volume 36, number 3 (September 1967), pp. 262–83, and reprinted in Richey and Jones, *American Civil Religion*, pp. 45–75. It is also a central essay in a book by Mead which takes its title from the essay (N.Y., 1975).

34. A good statement of this global universalism is: "[America's] synergistic cosmopolitanism lies at the heart of its nationalism—that a definitive element of the spiritual core which identifies it as a nation is the conception of a universal principle which is thought to transcend and include all the national and religious particularities brought to it by the people who come from all over the world to be 'Americanized.'" *Church History*, Volume 36, number 3 (September 1967), p. 273.

35. See Anthony F. C. Wallace, *Religion: An Anthropological View* (N.Y., 1966). Chapter Two, "The Anatomy of Religion," is especially relevant.

Epilogue

1. The phrase is the title of a book edited by Elwyn Smith, *The Religion of the Republic* (Philadelphia, 1971). Mead developed the phrase in his essay "The 'Nation with the Soul of a Church.'" Mead appropriated that title from G. K. Chesterton. Mead's essay originally appeared in *Church History*.

2. See especially Kenelm Burridge, *New Heaven, New Earth*.

3. See "Revitalization Movements," in *American Anthropologist*, Volume 58, pp. 264–81.

4. Insufficient attention has been given to this component of Bellah's original essay. See his concluding section, "The Third Time of Trial," in "Civil Religion in America," pp. 16–18, which echoes the Kennedy inaugural.

5. *Ibid.*, see especially note 1, p. 19.

Index